M000073778

Incarcerated: Escaping the Prison of Your Mind

Dr. Cecelia Martin, PhD

Incarcerated

Trilogy Christian Publishers
A Wholly Owned Subsidiary of Trinity Broadcasting Network
2442 Michelle Drive, Tustin, CA 92780

For information, address Trilogy Christian Publishing Rights Department, 2442 Michelle Drive, Tustin, CA 92780.

Trilogy Christian Publishing/ TBN and colophon are trademarks of Trinity Broadcasting Network.

For information about special discounts for bulk purchases, please contact Trilogy Christian Publishing.

Manufactured in the United States of America

Trilogy Disclaimer: The views and content expressed in this book are those of the author and may not necessarily reflect the views and doctrine of Trilogy Christian Publishing or the Trinity Broadcasting Network.

10 9 8 7 6 5 4 3 2 1
Library of Congress Cataloging-in-Publication Data is available.

ISBN: 978-1-68556-597-8
E-ISBN: 978-1-68556-598-5

Dedication

To my daughters, Tyler and Kennedy,
and my mom Linda.
I love you.

And to every bound soul, there is freedom.

Acknowledgements

First, I would like to thank my mother, Linda Joyce Freeman, the strongest woman I know, for all you have quietly suffered and endured. Thank you for allowing me to share a portion of your story with the world.

Thank you to my daughters—Tyler and Kennedy—for being honest critics and my biggest supporters. Without you, mommy could never do any of this. You are the most patient and understanding children ever to be born. God matched us perfectly.

To my brother Calvin, Jr., who is a better man than our father could ever be, I say with the utmost respect to our father, Calvin Simmons, Sr. Thank you for never giving up on me.

A huge thank you to DeAndrea Johnson for taking the writing journey with me, getting me organized, and pushing me to find my own voice. Because of your help, this body of work is a reality.

I am so grateful to my Aunt Mattie Howe for your love and transparency and for always being a bridge over troubled waters for the Simmons tribe.

Thank you to my childhood best friend Laynette Adams-Jacobs for supporting me through this gut-wrenching process and for laughing and crying with me always.

To every friend who has ever asked me to tell my story, here it is, in the raw, thanks for believing me. And finally, to my deeply flawed but loving father, Calvin Simmons, Sr., I know now that you did your best. Thank you for helping me to heal from within.

Special heartfelt blessings to TBN and Trilogy Publishing for partnering with me and letting my voice be heard.

Table of Contents

Preface: Touch

touch

/təCH/

verb

past tense: touched; past participle: touched

come into or be in contact with; bring one's hand
or another part of one's body into contact
with; come or bring into mutual contact; be
tangent to (a curve or surface) at a certain
point; handle in order to manipulate, alter, or
otherwise affect, especially in an adverse way.

As babies, we long to be touched. It's a natural desire from
the time we are born. "Hold me!" is found in the echo of
every cry from the crib. Frowned lips, balled up fists, a flood-
gate of tears roll in from the yearning to be touched. Feelings
of safety and love exude in the soothing touch of a parent.

But what happens when a child receives a touch that causes
anxiety and injects pain? The kind of touch that sours the soul
and suffocates all sense of love and security. An ungodly con-
nection that erases innocence and incriminates joy.

The touch becomes a never-ending reminder that something unusual happened that can never be erased. A touch
lingering, taking on a life of its own, shaping your develop-

ment, plaguing the mind. The type of touch that takes years to understand. It's remarkable how one single touch changed the course of my life.

Girls with Guitars

After twenty years, Linda and Joycelyn were together for the first time. It was an awkward but necessary situation. Linda didn't know how Joycelyn would receive her but was willing to take the risk of rejection if it meant she'd have a better life. She hadn't seen her mother Joycelyn since she was a baby. Her biological mother was a mere stranger who was abruptly forced to take her in as a living companion. It wasn't the ideal situation for either of them, but Linda was going to make it work. She had no other options.

Beep! Beep! Beep! Linda begrudgingly rolled onto her side. With her face half pressed against the pillow, she swatted the button of the clock for the second time. Ignoring the alarm once again, she retreated into the comforts of her bed and nestled the small of her back into the mattress for a few more seconds. Now staring at the white ceiling, hands resting on the center of her stomach, she exhaled. The cool fog of stale morning breath greeted her nostrils, triggering her memory that the window was still open from the night before. The sound of sirens wailing in the distance nearly overshadowed the short high-pitched squeak of the bus slipping onto the worn crevice of the street. The familiar sound of the metro doors swung open, ready to gulp the large group of people waiting at the stop. *I had better get up.* Linda tenderly released her bedsheets, dragging her body upward, and scooted to the edge of the bed.

Linda was 5'5 and never weighed much of anything. At a whopping hundred and ten pounds, she still maintained her girlish figure. That was ten pounds more than she had before giving birth. Joycelyn, just eighteen years older, somehow managed to keep an hourglass figure too after nine kids. Linda was the oldest of them. They said good genes run in the family. Except she had never known this side of the family.

After wiggling her toes into the blades of the plush throw rug, Linda pushed her fingers through her freshly permed hair, adjusted the straps of her tank top, and began a mental check-list of the day. *Milk, detergent, oatmeal, cheese slices... and I can't forget the trash.* Continuing about her morning routine, tending to her face, teeth, hair, she took another glance out the window before slamming it shut. With perfection, Linda quickly made her bed, fluffing the pillow, then pulling and tugging the com-forter to rid any sign of wrinkles. She grabbed her uniform from the closet but not before disposing of the half-eaten bowl of soup sitting on the nightstand from the night before. The plastic bowl clanked against the congregation of empty cups and beer cans as she tossed it into the trash can. It was an enjoyable sound after a long weekend with her brothers. Feeling anxious, she took another glimpse out the window to see if Joycelyn was waiting.

Joycelyn had left a few minutes early to start the car parked in the garage. The brown 1965 Chevy Chevelle belonged to Mr. and Mrs. Johnson, who lived across the hall in apartment number thirty-two. The young couple worked early mornings. Linda and Joycelyn were on the second shift. The Johnsons let them borrow their car two or three days out of the week to get to work, particularly when it was cold. They were good neighbors and looked out for each other. Linda and Joycelyn would borrow the car and, in return, kept it filled to the brim with gas for the young couple who was always trying to make ends meet.

"Oh, c'mon, not today, please start," Joycelyn pleaded with the car while giving it a crank. The Chevelle was a little worn but capable of making the trip to work if and when it started. Joycelyn rocked her foot back and forth on the gas a few more times, and *vroom, vroom.* "Ah yes, thank you!" She breathed a sigh of relief, briskly rubbed her hands together, then up and down her arms while giving the car time to heat.

Linda took another glance out the window and saw Joycelyn pull up near the alley. *There she is!* She snatched up the trash, her lunch bag, and her coat. "Thanks Mr. and Mrs. Johnson! Have a good day!" she yelled loudly while pulling and locking the door shut. Linda dropped the black bag of trash into the shoot then hurriedly walked down the hallway toward the elevator. Like most families in Washington, D.C., Linda and Joycelyn lived in a high-rise apartment, a building that was never quiet. The hypnotic beat of go-go music vibrated from one cracked windowpane to the next. Restless dogs barked at the sounds of planes flying overhead. Voices escalated in the hallways competing with the symphony of cars honking on the streets. The sound of television drama bellowed behind closed doors. Linda slowly grew accustomed to the sounds of urban life. It was easier to get used to than the cold. The weather was brutal compared to the never-ending summers in Texas. Even her heavy wool coat couldn't keep her warm enough as she exited the building into the alley. The breeze that lingered between the concrete structures always seemed to sneak up on her and catch her by surprise. She dashed out of the cold into the car.

They always left an hour early, which gave Linda enough time to take in the view. It never got old. *I can't believe I'm really here.* She was awestruck at the unlimited number of restaurants, storefront cafes, and street food vendors where well-dressed people stood in zombie-like fashion waiting to be brought to life with a another cup of joe. *I did it. I actually made it.* Linda really hadn't made it far enough. It was just the beginning of what would be a very long ride in her life. But for the moment, it was the most important milestone that she had accomplished, making it safely to Washington, D.C. with her children. *I wonder if she's happy that I'm here. I never dreamed I'd be riding to work with my actual mother. This is kind of nice.*

Joycelyn had both hands on the steering wheel, carefully navigating the crowded streets while Linda continued to take in the view. She delightfully gazed at the big afros and fitted bell-bottoms. Hipsters moved about; shoulders flanked with shirt collars resembling the wings of an aircraft. No one dressed like that in Diboll. The east coast was vastly different from the quiet town where she grew up, that's for sure. The District of Columbia was bustling and vibrant. The mostly flat, sometimes hilly sidewalks of the chocolate city were flooded with people. The gray sidewalks that wound around the city were a novelty too. There wasn't much need for concrete pathways in the small town of Diboll, (pronounced Die-ball) Texas.

Joycelyn pulled up to the office gate and flashed her badge through the car window at the security guard. Linda was still counting her blessings. *Man, I'm really lucky. If my mother hadn't gotten me this job, I don't know what I would've done,* she thought with a heart full of gratitude.

After a few minutes of fishing for a parking spot in the poorly light garage, circling one level after the next, Joycelyn stuffed the faithful Chevelle in a narrow parking space. They entered the building and took the elevator to the tenth floor to clock in. As usual, Linda began her nearly perfect cleaning routine. She dusted the furniture, desks, and chairs, emptied the wastebaskets, and left the vacuuming for last. While wiping traces of fingerprints from the windows, she paused, as she often did from time to time to watch girls her age, walking carefree. Linda longed to know where they were going. Some of the women were dressed in blazers and miniskirts, with scarves tied around their neck and carrying designer handbags. *Humph, Papa would kill me if he ever saw me dressed like that.* Maybe they were going shopping, or to a fancy event, she imagined. Then there were the ladies that walked slowly hand in hand with a man, strolling under the big open sky, seemingly with the one they loved. "Linda, what are you doing? Are you finished? Let's go." Joycelyn called out from down the hallway.

"I'm coming," Linda broke her trance before heading back to the tenth floor to clock out for the evening. Just as she was about to reach the elevator, she paused to grab the last bag of trash left in the hallway and noticed a dim light still on in one of the offices. Peeking through the cracked door, she saw a woman seated at one of the desks. She had never seen a woman behind a desk doing paperwork. *What is she doing?* The woman appeared to be working in the office but wasn't cleaning or vacuuming the floor. She wore makeup, expensive shoes, and professional clothes. Linda was perplexed. Tilting her head and squinting, she turtled her neck a little further through the door to make sure she wasn't dreaming. *I want to do whatever she is doing. I want to work behind a desk, too.* Before that day, Linda had no aspirations whatsoever, didn't have a dream or desire to be anything, she didn't even know what it meant *to be*. Her curiosity and independence were held hostage inside the intimate town and small trailer home where she was raised. There was no exposure to other forms of being in Diboll. She was simply destined to be whatever her parents were. For the first time, the gray scales of her mind had fallen off. She wanted to do something with her life and suddenly realized she had options for her future. *I made it this far. Surely, I can figure out a way to work at a desk,* she was convinced.

When Linda arrived in the District of Columbia, she didn't want to impose or be a burden to anyone. She just wanted to find a job that paid enough money for food, pampers, milk, the minimum necessities to take care of toddlers. Thankfully it wasn't long before Joycelyn got her a job working as an office cleaner. To some, being a cleaning lady might seem like a mediocre job, but she was happy and proud to be a custodian. Cleaning was a part of the family legacy. Her mother was a domestic hand, and her grandmother was "the help" and worked for affluent whites, taking care of their house and children. Now, she was a custodian in a big city building. There was a genuine sense of pride in keeping with the tradition of the women in her family. And she loved earning her own money. Linda was a simple hard-working woman who was neutral about life in general. Not optimistic or overly expectant, but she held tight to her humble roots and was eager to fulfill the role meticulously engineered for her through her upbringing. That meant becoming an outstanding custodian. But all of that changed when she saw the woman sitting at the desk.

Another successful shift had ended, so Linda and Joycelyn drove back to the apartment. Pausing in front of a nearby convenience store, Jocelyn remembered that Linda needed to gather a few things for the evening. "Linda, you have your list darling?" Joycelyn always communicated with the tone and cadence of an heiress. It was her way of ridding any shred of evidence that she was originally from a small country town.

"Yes ma'am. I know exactly what I need. I won't be long."

"Okay dear, I'll wait out here and keep the car running."

The winter hawk nipped mercilessly at Linda's pale, scrawny legs as she ran into the store holding her wool jacket shut over her stained uniform and work satchel. It took just five minutes or so to get milk, detergent, oatmeal, and cheese slices. She placed her items on the counter and reached into her purse while fidgeting from the cool wind that continued to sweep in with each new customer that entered the door.

"That'll be $4.30," the cashier said while bagging the items.

Linda rummaged through her purse and checked her spare pocket. "Here, I have $4.10," extending her arm as if to present her counteroffer to the cashier.

"Well, do you want to put something back? I can take off the cheese slices if you like," the cashier was unwilling to negotiate.

"But I need everything on my list. Don't y'all run a tab? I can pay you at the end of the week?" There were only two places to get groceries in Diboll. One was part of a growing grocery chain, the other, Tanners, owned by the Tanner family. Both stores let regulars run a tab as long as it was settled by the end of the month.

The cashier laughed in utter disbelief, "Honey child, I know you not serious."

Linda insisted, "But I come in here at least once a week, you know I'm good for it."

Joycelyn, now impatient, taps the horn twice to remind Linda she's waiting in a no-park zone. The woman next in line started to get annoyed, sighing loudly and began to mutter while rolling her eyes at Linda's ignorance. After some consideration, Linda decided cheese was somewhat of a luxury, so she left the store without it.

As the days passed, Linda carried on her routine with Joycelyn: getting dressed for work, making the bed, making sandwiches for lunch; two slices of bread, Miracle Whip, bologna, unfortunately, no cheese. Each time she arrived at work, she carried in her mind the image of the woman at the desk. The vivid picture interrupted her coarse manufactured thoughts about what women could do in the workplace. Inspired and determined, she began asking questions and was told the woman she saw was a secretary and there was a special training school for women who wanted to work in an office. Without hesitation, Linda applied to school and was accepted. The program guaranteed an interview once she finished her classes. As promised, the school delivered and scheduled a meeting with the National Labor Relations Board. Linda landed her first administrative job with a good government agency and gained a brand-new lease on life. She couldn't wait to call home and share the news with May and Papa.

Now instead of watching other women from the office building, Linda was one of those women living the city life, working full-time, and relishing in her independence. Her new taste of freedom meant one day getting her own apartment and breaking some of the restrictions from her childhood that she continued to self-impose. Dancing was one of those restricted things she didn't do growing up in Papa's house, but Joycelyn, Linda, and her younger eight siblings loved to dance! Linda lived with her mother, Joycelyn, and three of her five brothers. Each of her two sisters had a place of their own across town. Mom had never spent time with any of her siblings when she was a child. Papa wouldn't allow it. Although she was no longer with Papa, like the endless sidewalks around the city and the freedom to dance, having brothers and sisters was a novelty.

For the most part, it had always been just the three of us: me, my mom Linda, and my brother Junior. But when we moved to D.C., we had aunts, uncles, and cousins. It was nice to be around a large family. We were particularly fond of our crazy uncles. They were a rowdy bunch, playing cards all night while drinking, smoking, and talking nonsense. My uncles took jabs at each other until the wee hours of the morning, but it was all in wholesome fun. By the time the sun was up, the tiny apartment had reeked of stale beer and smoldered cigarettes. Still, the togetherness of family and the magnetic energy of having relatives around is what lingered in my memory the most.

Where there was family, there was always music. Music was different on the east coast and had taken on an even newer sound. There was no shortage of funky, eclectic hits, and everyone was grooving. A band called A Taste of Honey was burning the airwaves, singing everyone into the "Boogie Oogie Oogie." One night, the all-girl singing group was on the television, and to my shock, the women were black, playing electric guitars. A crowd of people of all colors danced, popping their hips in all directions with no fixed movements, just impulsive expressions to the music. They hopped, and some rapidly flapped their elbows, arms swinging across the body, feet motioning back and forth. Men with half-buttoned shirts pointed their fingers while jerking in a seizure-like fashion, swinging their heads from left to right. As soon as the beat of the "Boogie Oogie Oogie" started, my uncles began their grove, "*Hay,* they are funky, those girls are off the hook." One uncle had a cigarette gently perched between his fingers, another obscurely cuddling a newly opened can of ice-cold beer, as they shuffled across the congested living room floor. I was glued to the television screen, standing, eyes wide, mouth gaping, fascinated, and captivated by the beautiful copper-skinned women and their electric guitars. "One day, I'm going to play the electric guitar," I fondly imagined.

Gathered around the television with me were my brother and our playmate Aunt Sabrina. Aunt Sabrina was the youngest of my mother's three sisters and the same age as Junior and me. Grandmother Joycelyn nearly died of shock when she found out she was pregnant with baby number nine. It must have been devastating to discover she was having a child that late in life. But it was great for us because Aunt Sabrina was the only other person our age who was consistently around for jacks, hopscotch, and jump rope. And she and Junior entered into full karaoke mode when the soulful sounds of Funkadelic, The Jackson 5, and Donna Summer came on. As for me, I preferred the roaring sounds of Journey, Aerosmith, Rod Stewart, and that "Old Time Rock and Roll," you know, "the kind of music that soothes the soul…" There was something so freeing and exhilarating in the sound. Watching rock stars perform on television was exciting. Everything was so offbeat, making me feel I could lose myself in the music. The wild hair, flamboyant outfits, smoke rising from the stage made it even more tantalizing. *If there is a heaven,* I thought, *I'm going to be a rock star when I get there! I'm going to play an electric guitar, bang my head back and forth and sing to the roar of the heavenly host!*

The fantasy always took root for at least a good ten minutes. I'd be wearing black biker boots, bold bell sleeves extending at the wrist. You know, the kind of blouse the Artist Formerly Known as Prince used to wear. The wind would ripple through the layers of my ankle-length polyester jacket. My knee-length scarves wave in the air like rags clutched to a clothesline. My regal, larger-than-life hair would bobble above my head, hug the flaps of my ears, and wrap around my neck as I prepared to belt. I'd slowly approach the microphone. Shoulders squared, feet firmly planted, and with a forceful grip I'd wring the neck of my guitar with one hand, and swing in one pitcher's motion downward and forward with the other. My back reclining to the stance of an old La-Z-Boy, immediately the dramatic riff of my guttural strum would vibrate through the heavens with a Panasonic boom. Hundreds of thousands flood into the golden east gate, all chanting, fists pumping with enthusiasm, "Holy is the Lord! Holy, holy, holy!" Celebrating in tempo to my angelic metallic sound. Okay, a girl can dream, can't she!

I admit we never went to a church in D.C., and even still, I don't think there would have been a rock and roll band there. I'd heard all about heaven and hell, salvation and angels from television and radio preachers. My favorite was Billy Graham. I was especially fond of him because he was so matter of fact about the Bible, sure and unyielding about every word. He had a way of making you feel both lost and found all at the same time. And there was something so soothing about the cadence of his voice. It was strong yet full of compassion. The power of his convictions was magnified and evident in how he held the Bible and moved his hands. He preached as if he was a father to everyone and was on an eager mission to put us on the right path. Before ending his sermons, he reminded everyone about a very important decision about Jesus that needed to be made. It never occurred to me that I, too would one day have to make a choice, that I would one day need to accept or reject the resurrection power of Jesus the Christ.

He Touched Me

My mom was never the warm, touchy-feely type. She didn't cut sandwiches into little animal shapes or kiss our boo-boos after a fall. There were no daily words of affirmation and certainly no cuddling or stroking. We didn't wait with anticipation to be tucked in at night in hopes of hearing a magical bedtime story. And lullabies? Well, that's just laughable. She wasn't *that kind* of mother. Mom had no illusions of gentleness. Instead, she exuded an extraordinary amount of grit and discipline like that of a skilled bodybuilder bench pressing under the excruciating weight of life. She loved us, without question, in her own way, but she was a child who was raising children. Her expressions of love were embedded in her actions, evident in the clean clothes we wore, the obsessive way she kept things organized, and the many times she stayed home with us rather than prance around the city with other young people her age. But the true testament of her love was her relentless commitment to care and provide for us, on her own, without the help of our father or her grandparents, Papa and May.

Nearly six or seven years had passed while we were in Washington, D.C., and our father only sent for us once. Other than that, he never sent us gifts or called. Like any little girl, I always longed to have my daddy, and it was painfully obvious to me that I was without him. I envied other little girls walking down the street holding their daddy's hand or when I saw them mounted on their father's shoulders in the park. I wanted to be up high, too, and to feel the security of my daddy's formidable hands gripping my ankles. Those little girls had a different view of the world because there was no hint of fear of falling in their eyes. They'd spread their arms wide like an airplane and pretend to fly or securely pin their hands to their daddy's neck. With a face full of joy, they'd perhaps clutch onto his ears, and I'd watch their father chuckle and squirm with slight discomfort, but he'd hold on anyway and carry them for as long as he could. I wanted that; I wanted my daddy to carry me.

Things were going well for Mom at work, and she eventually saved enough money to get a two-bedroom apartment of her own. Unfortunately for Junior and me, the new apartment came with an eviction notice. My brother and I were being evicted out of Mom's personal space and into our own bedroom. The three of us had slept together for years. But as we grew, Mom complained of being kicked, poked, and prodded during the night. So our days of nestling underneath her maternal wings were over.

The modest apartment wasn't a spacious condo or a house, but it was perfect for us. We had a plush navy-blue couch that converted to a pullout bed. It sat in the center of the living room on the faux hardwood floors. We sometimes aggravated the tenets beneath us with the ruckus of chasing each other around. Adjacent to the wide balcony in our high-rise apartment was a cozy U-shaped kitchen that captured the breeze as it swept over the round wooden eating table. The box-shaped bedrooms had cool tan walls and a white popcorn ceiling, making the rooms feel larger than they actually were. It was initially hard for us to sleep in a separate room from Mom. We took turns gingerly tiptoeing back and forth from our room to hers, hoping to get an invitation to climb in her bed, with no such luck. Other times we'd just talk to each other from across the room about cartoons, toys, and the usual nothingness kids ramble about until eventually falling asleep. There was a tangible feeling of safety when I slept at night, and goodness existed in my surroundings. I laughed without reservation, had no fear of a monster crawling under my bed. I was free, unrestricted, basking in the light of purity.

Then one evening, on the rare occasion mom went out with one of her girlfriends, she asked Uncle Hunter to come over. Uncle Hunter was tall, like a basketball player. He had milk chocolate -colored skin, perfect teeth, and a broad smile. His thick shoulders complimented his medium chest and trim waistline. He was my favorite uncle and was a good cook, too.

"I'm gonna cook for you and your brother tonight."

"What you gonna make Uncle?"

"You'll see."

I pulled up a chair and never took my eyes off the stove. My interest amused him. He filled a pot with water and waited for it to boil, then heated a pan to brown some ground beef.

"Spaghetti!" My favorite meal. Uncle Hunter popped open a few cans, and it wasn't long before the aroma of tomato sauce began to circulate. I sat in the chair barefoot, legs swinging, waiting for him to finish his masterpiece. And finally, it was ready.

"Y'all come on and eat."

We scurried to the table, and I could hardly wait for Uncle Hunter to serve us our plates. I jammed my fork into the center of the sauce, using both hands to twirl the fork into the noodles. Then slurped a mouthful of the spaghetti, puckering in any straggling noodles, until my jaws were chowing through the al dente pasta like a chipmunk. I licked the corners of my mouth, cautious not to lose a drop of sauce. It was delicious as usual.

Once dinner was over, we were allowed to watch television before bed. Uncle Hunter had unfolded the pullout couch while we were eating, so we could rest while watching television. I climbed in. Junior remained on the floor with his back propped against the side of the frame. We were wholly engrossed in a Jerry Lewis classic, *The Disorderly Orderly*. With full stomachs and tired eyes, we laughed and yawned and laughed some more. I acquiesced to the ease of what felt like a perfectly peaceful night and fell asleep. I was comfortably resting when I was disturbed by a touch, an uncommon closeness from Uncle Hunter.

At first, I thought I was dreaming. But then I awakened enough to hear the TV still on in the background. I assumed my brother had gone to bed, and Uncle Hunter was about to pick me up and put me in mine. Then Hunter reached for me again in a way I could not ignore. I didn't think much of it at first. But there was something strange and sinister about his actions. I had no point of reference for what was happening or why. So, I lay motionless, paralyzed at my core. Thoughts scattered through my brain like a bed of fire ants. I kept my eyes closed and could not make sense of what was happening. *What is Uncle Hunter doing? Is something wrong with me? Did I do something? Where is Junior?* "Please, don't. Dear God!" Something took over, and I quickly jolted into a faraway place in my mind.

> *I grab my guitar, I play real it loud,*
> *The strings of the metal will cover the sound.*
> *I know where I am, and where I will be,*

And nothing can damage my soul in the sea.
My soul is an ocean, and I am the waves,
My heart is a rock. My mind is a cave.

My heart hammered inside of my body. My stomach turned, and my soul quivered as I continued to play possum. I kept my eyes closed and remained completely silent. My brother was fast asleep in our bedroom and never knew what happened.

At that moment, I became keenly aware that something essential was conspicuously missing from my life. I reflected on the fathers who carried their daughters on their shoulders. A new consciousness deepened the void that had always been present. I was a product of gross neglect, not from my mother but from my father. He was supposed to keep me safe in this world. Call it instinct or natural inclination, but I expected my father, a man, to rescue me from being violated by another man. I reflected on the fathers who carried their daughters on their shoulders. I needed him to protect me. I didn't know where my father was but immediately felt the consequences of his absence. Hunter's heinous acts transmitted a clear signal to my psyche that I was uncovered and without protection.

For months on end, instead of being open, free, and full of joy, I was numb and despondent. Suddenly, everything around me was magnified. The world was eerie and dark, and I was held captive in it. I was cloaked in shame and became paranoid and jittery around adults. I didn't want to be around other kids either. The sound of laughter was offensive and a direct insult to my pain. My entire reason for living was in question, including why God allowed something so sickening to happen to me.

The God I heard about on the television was inherently good to all people. And if God was indeed benevolent, then I must have done something wrong. Or maybe what happened was normal. My private thoughts consumed me and set in motion a pattern of thinking that I could not control.

The age of innocence for a child seems short-lived as it is, so to have it cut even shorter for any reason is criminal. The knowledge of good and evil, while inevitable, should not be the norm. There is no sadder scenario than when innocence is stolen from a child. Carrying the secret of what Uncle Hunter had done slowly and steadily hardened my heart. Over time I became easily irritated and combative when I was around adults. I later turned defiant towards my mom for not knowing what happened to me, bitter with my father for not being there, and mad at God for my existence.

Malice

For Mom, things were good, but living in D.C. grew tough after a few years. It seemed like her new lease on life was up. The cost of living was high, and she was no longer making enough money to take care of the three of us. She had a secure job, but it was entry-level. And it bothered her to sit in the office doing the same work for less pay. The white secretaries were advancing and living the American dream. She'd hear them in the break room discussing their husbands and homes or the expensive toys they bought for their kids. Mom didn't have a husband or a house. She was barely making ends meet for us. It was one thing for her to struggle, but she wanted to create more stability for Junior and me. She decided it would be best to leave Washington, D.C., and move back to Texas, where the cost of living was cheaper. If she stayed with May and Papa for a while, she would have time to get her footing and figure out her next move.

But returning to Diboll would be like returning to a small jail cell. Although she had proven that she could live on her own, she still wouldn't have the ability to function as an adult living under Papa's roof. With some reservation, she grabbed the suitcases and started packing. *There would be no dating and no parties,* she thought, as she poured the last bottle of vodka down the kitchen sink. *The three of us will have to go back to sharing a bed for a while,* she was not looking forward to that. *And I'd have to start dressing according to Papa's standards,* so she placed her high heel shoes and miniskirts in a bag to gift to

Mrs. Johnson across the hall. Going back was a hard decision but a much needed turning point in her life. Home was where she needed to be. Mom and Joycelyn said their goodbyes at the bus station, uncertain if they'd ever see each other again.

The energy drained from my mom's once glowing face and bright eyes when we moved back to Diboll. She was disappointed that nothing had advanced or changed. Diboll was claustrophobic and was more of a small neighborhood, unlike the bustling city we used to live in. Everything was just as we left it. Oddly, for me, there was something comforting about the familiarity and predictability of it all. Diboll was tucked away and offered the illusion of safety. Tanners, the makeshift family-owned store, was still in walking distance, just a stone's throw away. The honeysuckle in front of the old graveyard still blossomed and harbored caterpillars, and the suckle was still just as sweet. We could still outrun the cargo train near the edge of town that never gained any additional speed; it still crept down the tracks. And as usual, folks wandered onto the porch when an unfamiliar car drove through, my great-grandparents included. May was still lovable and worrisome, and unfortunately, Papa hadn't changed either. He was still terrifying.

My great-grandfather's name was Romalice Freeman; we called him Papa. Everyone else referred to him as Malice, a name worthy of his distinctive aura. Papa's presence echoed throughout the tiny dim trailer home like a whale suffocating in a pool. Years of intense disappointment lingered in his eyes. Fragmented dreams lined the frame of his countenance and clung to his silhouette. He was immensely tall with a slight hunch in his shoulders. The shadow of Papa's sorrow was always painfully evident by the still picture resting on his face.

His finely chiseled cheekbones guarded any hint of a smile, and the appearance or sound of laughter never parted his lips. The residue of life rested underneath the boards of his coarse yellow fingernails. The veins in his hands stretched through his charcoal-colored skin like the roots of an old oak tree. Something had happened to him. He was stern, authoritative, and emanated intimidation. Papa was a mean man, and no one in Diboll was ever going to challenge or meddle with the likes of him. The whispers around town were that he never recovered from the loss of his first wife and son, who both died of tuberculosis. He was left to raise his daughter Joycelyn alone, without his wife and companion nor a son to carry his name.

Papa was never one to initiate or go looking for trouble, yet his calloused palms were known for toting a gun or two. A rifle was always within his reach. And if you ever got out of line, those same rustic hands would be inclined to immediately dispense a good beating. He was known for his lack of tolerance and excessive discipline. There was no negotiating with him. The best way to communicate or deal with Papa was through May.

Papa remarried Mable, my great-grandmother. All the children called her May. Although May and Papa never had a child together, May became a loving mother to Joycelyn. Joycelyn sometimes found herself at odds with May and in near-death experiences with Papa because of her disobedience. Sadly, the stricter Papa became, the more Joycelyn reached towards the outside world. She became promiscuous and was pregnant with my mom, Linda, by age seventeen. Papa was furious and not at all forgiving. He took his shotgun and threatened the father, Ben, within an inch of his life. Dreading Papa's rage, Ben joined the Air Force and never again returned to Diboll. Joycelyn was left to give birth to her first child alone, and without consultation, Papa took Mom from Joycelyn when she was just an infant.

When Joycelyn arrived home from the hospital, Papa minced no words about who would raise my mom, Linda. "Joycelyn, you give that baby to Mable and go wash dem dishes. Don't you be thinkin' you gone raise no child round here," he said with sternness in his voice. "And when you done wid those dishes, get out dere and pick some mustard greens for dinner."

Joycelyn did not put up a fight. She knew better than to challenge him. Joycelyn did as she was told while May embraced all the joys of being a new mother. May inhaled the sweetness of her baby's breath. May, not Joycelyn, held, fed, and rocked her to sleep. When mom was old enough to say her first words, she called May "Mama." And that is how things remained. "Mama" was reserved for May and May alone, and she never ever referred to anyone else as such, not even her own mother, Joycelyn.

Back in those days, grandparents just took children and raised them if they saw fit. No one involved the courts or child protective services in private family matters. Grandmother Joycelyn eventually left May and Papa and moved into a home just two miles away. Still, mom was never allowed to stay with her or visit. Eventually, Grandmother Joycelyn fled to Washington, D.C., with the father of child number five and left Diboll for good, leaving my mother behind. Joycelyn wrote letters or called on occasion, but neither Joycelyn nor Ben had the courage to go back to Diboll to take their daughter back even though they were well within their rights to do so. They feared Papa too much to challenge his decision.

Mom wasn't shy about letting us know she, too, feared Papa more than she feared God. Her extreme fear of him was warranted. Certain memories were at the forefront of her mind. The insignia of Papa's authority had seared like scorching brass pressed against the flesh of a prized cattle. Mom would recall the day when Grandmother Joycelyn came by to have a talk with Papa.

Joycelyn sauntered in the house, "Hey Papa."

Papa remained seated with a neutral expression on his face, "What you come round here for," he responded.

"Uh, sir. Well, I wanted to talk to you about Linda. And how come you still keepin' my child. I'm old enough to take care of her myself now."

Papa leaned to grab the snuff can from the side of the chair and spit into it, "Linda ain't goin nowhere wid you."

"But Papa, she's my daughter," Joycelyn said in a strained tone.

No one can remember the rest of the conversation, only that Joycelyn was determined to express her honest opinions. But Papa perceived that she was being flippant toward him. He slowly rose from his chair with a look of indignation. And before anyone could blink, Papa had grabbed an ashtray stand and, with a venomous force, struck Joycelyn across the forehead. The collective gasp sucked all the air from the room. Mom and May stood slack jawed as Joycelyn's hands grappled for the air, but there was nothing to break her fall. Her feet slipped from beneath her. She flew backward, and her body slammed to the floor. Eight months pregnant with her third child, at the sound of the thud, her belly flopped and jiggled on impact. She lay unconscious, and no one could tell whether or not she was breathing. But no one dared make a move toward her. Thankfully, Grandmother Joycelyn was breathing and did eventually wake. She survived, the baby was unharmed, and most importantly, she lived to tell of her insurrection.

Papa was just that mean, but we loved him dearly. I loved him. I don't know why he was so rigid and withdrawn. No one knows. But he was, in many respects, the only father my mother had ever known and the only father figure in my life at that time. His very presence was like a fortress. I was never afraid that he would touch me or allow me to be touched. People knew that there was a man in the house who would keep us safe or would surely die trying. He was one of those complicated figures.

On the one hand, you knew Papa wouldn't let anything harm you, and on the other, some things you didn't share with Papa if you didn't want blood on your hands. You trusted and respected him, but you didn't run to tell him your troubles either. It would be like launching nuclear codes. Papa had to be the last resort, if you wanted to rid your problem for good. For better or for worse, Papa was the man and role model in all of our lives.

Papa didn't have much family around except for his sister Kaylee. Aunt Kaylee and her husband Joe lived in Diboll too. He worked at the sawmill, May was a housekeeper, and when the days ran long, Aunt Kaylee and Uncle Joe would look after Mom. Aunt Kaylee was independent in every way. She was wild, cursed like a sailor, and drank like one too. She was always working and often sweaty. Her galaxy black skin beamed in the country sunlight. The bangs of her hair plummeted just above the brow. She wasn't shy about anything and never lost eye contact while telling her profanity-laced stories. Imagine, it's the annual family cookout. A woman struts to the picnic table to join the group of wives dressed in their pristine tablecloth dresses and white gloves. She tilts her sunglasses and begins an undomesticated dialogue with a beer in hand, raving to all the housewives about her entrepreneurial pursuits. "I want to invite all you ladies to my cafe. Business is booming," she rambles on, using choice words and street talk, while the women clutch their pearls. Aunt Kaylee was known for her rambunctious personality, no signs of being docile, a woman well before her time.

Mom enjoyed staying with Aunt Kaylee because she broke all the rules. "Linda, I know'd Malice don't allow you ta listen to no music. But you's a young gurl and I don't see nothin' wrong wid it. You gone enjoy yoself when you wid me. Ya here?" Music and dancing were, and still are, my mom's secret love. Mom wasn't allowed to dance in Papa's house. But Aunt Kaylee and Uncle Joe had the remedy to Papa's restrictions because their cafe had music. People throughout the town would secretly bop down through the worn trail in the dark woods to Joe's Cafe to relieve their stress and dance their troubles away. Joe's Café wasn't just a place for adults to let loose, but a keepsake in the community, always at the center of every football victory, weekend family gathering, and seasonal holiday party.

Aunt Kaylee kept the little juke joint stocked with sodas, cookies, potato chips, ice cream, candy, all the tempting goodies for children and adults alike. Mom loved when the handyman would tune the Victrola record player and clean the turntables when the café was closed. He'd let the records play one after another to ensure the machine was working correctly, Ray Charles, The Chiffons, Sam Cooke. Mom would "cut a rug," as the old folks would say, swiftly moving her feet, twirling about. The big dance floor was a little piece of heaven on earth. Sadly, Mom lost her secret place when Uncle Joe had a sudden, untimely heart attack. Aunt Kaylee was too overwhelmed with the upkeep of the business after he died, so she closed the café and moved to a farm in Nigton.

Nigton was another small town twenty miles west of Diboll. Papa would take the family there from time to time to check on Aunt Kaylee and feed the hogs he was raising on her farm. The red dirt road to Nigton wasn't safe to travel at night. There were no lights, and sometimes an animal would dash out of the tall grass and into the road. The pitch-black darkness was ominous and frightening. So we always left just before dawn when it was time to visit Aunt Kaylee. Just as the tip of the morning sun kissed the edge of the sky, while the rooster performed its morning serenade, Papa would stand in the hallway and announce, "Linda, I'm gone be ready to get up yonder to Nigton in a minute." Then he'd grab the first slop bucket in the kitchen, walk down the steps leading to the back yard, take the sticky handle of the other old rusty slop barrel and carefully load them onto the back of his baby blue pickup truck. The fermented food swayed with his every movement, creating an unforgettable distinct gloppy sound. He'd methodically place the cans between two wooden boards so they wouldn't slip or tilt over on our bumpy ride. My Mom, brother, and I would hop in the cabin of the truck. My brother was usually pressed in the middle of the worn leather seat while I sat on my mom's lap. We'd continue down the road, me leaning on the front of the dash with my mom's arms wrapped around my tiny waist, my brother peering out the windshield. We'd travel the long dusty road, mostly in silence. Papa didn't talk much. What would he say anyway, should he choose to speak? What do you say to a little girl who has been stripped of any possibility of knowing her parents? How do you justify the choice to interfere and cut the natural bond of a lion and her cub? No one will ever comprehend it, and they all stopped trying to make sense of it. It's just the way things were. Although Grandmother Joycelyn, in essence, was a child herself when she gave birth, something is disturbing and cruel about a little girl not being able to see her mom, father, brothers, and sisters.

Papa didn't listen to music but patiently searched the radio signal for a baseball game or the news station. But the trips to Nigton were mainly filled with silence. Papa would strike up a conversation on rare occasions, but not before grabbing his snuff can from the floor console to take a spit.

"Linda, you know they say that boy 'round Clark's place done died of a heart attack. Left two chillen." He'd continue about what funeral home had the body and where the man would be buried. Papa didn't really have a conversation; it was more of an update or his way of reminding my mom of things she needed to do.

"Linda, when we get back to the house, make sure you help Mable take dem dere vegetables from the garden down to Mrs. Scott's place," he'd say.

"Yes, sir," she'd reply, in a quiet, reserved voice. In many ways, Mom became the son Papa didn't have anymore. She was expected to do things like haul the groceries from the store, make repairs around the house, and help Papa fix the car. Mom felt cheated of her childhood to a great extent, not just because she had babies at such a young age, but because Papa never loosened the reins and choked the youth out of her.

Kids Raising Kids

Mom was one of the first three black girls to integrate the all-white high school in town, Diboll High. To her surprise, she had no problems getting along with her white classmates. An invisible wall between the whites and blacks kept interaction civil. Each group had its own social circles and separate football teams. They even had their own homecoming king and queen.

School was the one soft spot for Papa when it came to giving Mom a little breathing room. He didn't meddle too much when Mom had things to do at school. He allowed her to do extracurricular activities. If her grades were in check, Mom was guaranteed those few extra hours to be around other kids. She played basketball and later joined the high school band. When she joined band, she learned to read sheet music and play the clarinet. The band was the only group to be fully integrated. Blacks and whites came together to make music, and that's when she discovered that it was possible to work together with others even if they had opposing views. She loved wearing the band uniform, attending the games with friends, and being away from home. The freedom was exhilarating, and she began to break out of her shell. That's when she met my dad, Calvin Simmons, Sr, and his sister Bonnie.

My father was the typical jock and always left a trail of whispering girls behind as he walked through the halls. He was medium height, incredibly petite, and the son of the most famous pastor in town. Everyone knew him as Reverend

Simmons' boy. Rev, as we called him, was a well-known, highly respected pastor of a Baptist church. Being a preacher's kid was a big deal; it meant instant notoriety. People around town held ministers in high regard, which meant the preacher's children always got a little extra attention and grace. "Oh Calvin, you don't have your homework again today. Well, just bring it tomorrow and can you please ask Reverend Simmons to pray for my husband, he's got a terrible flu," the teachers were never shy about plugging in a prayer request.

Reverend Simmons was known for taking care of his flock and feeding the children of God as if he were the father himself. Yet his own kids, well they were hard to handle at times. His daughter, Bonnie, was wild in Mom's eyes, something she loved and gravitated toward. Bonnie knew about boys, danced, and even went to parties! Mom couldn't imagine that life. Bonnie was so outspoken and playful. She was always trying to get mom further out of her shell and into a little trouble. "Hey Linda, the football team is going to park after the game, you comin'? It's gonna be a lot of fun! You know how the boys are after the game," Bonnie would say with a sly, flirtatious grin. But there was only so far Mom could push the limits with Papa. She wasn't willing to take those types of risks.

Even though they were different, Bonnie and my mom became close friends by default. They needed each other. Mom was shy, but Bonnie had street smarts, a skill my mom lacked profoundly. Bonnie was a fun-loving free spirit, and Mom was the voice of caution and reason when Bonnie wanted to take things too far. They spent a lot of time together, and that's when Bonnie's brother Calvin started to notice. "Linda, my brother wants to know if you'll sit with him in the cafeteria today,"

Bonnie said with a snicker. She had already set her mind to make Mom Calvin's girlfriend. With Bonnie's cunning ways and matching-making skills, it wasn't long before Mom and Dad became high school sweethearts. Mom was thrown into the deep end. She had no experience with boys. So, Bonnie became Mom's self-appointed tutor and taught Mom to flirt and be more appealing and how to "handle" a boy like Calvin.

It wasn't long before they began sneaking around. Neither wanted Papa to find out they were together. When Calvin walked Mom home after practice, he'd go as far as he could to remain out of sight. Bonnie would remind Mom to "walk slowly and don't forget to hold his hand." Bonnie also became the official watchman and lookout when mom and Calvin were at their house for a few moments alone. Unfortunately, there were too many moments alone, and before long, Mom found herself pregnant during her senior year. Seventeen and pregnant is a nightmare for anyone, but for Mom, well, it could be the end when Papa found out. At the first inclination that she might be pregnant, she was too terrified to say anything to May or Papa, and my father Calvin feared for his life. He wanted to confirm that Mom was indeed pregnant. So, he drove her to another nearby town to take a blood test.

"Well Linda, if you are pregnant, you know Rev is going to make us get married," he said as if trying to reassure her.

"I know," mom was mute, at a loss for words.

"But I don't mind, I reckon I was gonna marry you anyway. I love you, Linda. I'm going to take care of you and the baby. I ain't turnin' away from what's mine," trying to reassure her once again that no matter the outcome, all would be well. But it wasn't well for Mom. The pregnancy test was positive.

Needing time for the reality to set in, neither of them planned to tell anybody. They agreed only to confess the obvious once her belly grew out far enough. But that didn't matter. Whether or not they wanted to wait to break the news, after Mom started eating bowls of uncooked oatmeal and salted raw potatoes dipped in vinegar, it didn't take May long to realize what was happening. "My Lord Linda, you're pregnant," May muttered at the kitchen table. Mom looked somberly at May, signaling shock and shame. Without saying a word, their eyes slowly surveilled the living room where Papa was sitting, and both breathed a sigh of relief to see him nodding in the chair. Mom and May walked lighter than usual around the house for the next several months, afraid to let the secret show.

Calvin had never met Papa before and continued to take extra precautions to stay out of sight. Until one day, Calvin pulled up to the yard. May was sitting on the porch, shucking peas. Mom whispered to May, "Mama, that's Calvin. He's the one who got me pregnant."

"Malice!" May yelled through the cracked window. "Rev. Simmons' boy is here, I thank he's wantin' ta see you," she motioned toward the front door, instructing Calvin to pause and wait outside until she sent for him. Calvin stood still, quiet, focused, looking as if he was about to walk the plank or head for the guillotine. Mom didn't say anything either. The two lost puppies stood in the center of the yard, and after a few minutes, May returned and invited Calvin in. Mom looked over at Calvin, then bowed her head, "You can come on in now Calvin, Malice will see ya. Linda, you stay out here while these men folk talk for a spell," Mom's body started to tremble.

Calvin walked slowly through the front door. "Uh, hello Mr. Freeman." Papa remained seated and didn't return any pleasantries.

"What you want boy," he responded while seeming to peer right through his soul.

"I wanted to talk to you about Linda."

"Rev know you round here?" Papa asked with a stern grit in his voice.

"Yes sir, Rev knows I'm here," Calvin tried to keep his voice steady.

Mom was not allowed to hear the discussion, but Calvin asked Papa for her hand in marriage. Unbeknownst to her, there was a trial, judge, and jury taking place in the house, and Mom was about to be sentenced. She was never told the details of the conversation or whether Calvin or May told Papa about the pregnancy. The verdict was in, and to her shock, she was instantly engaged to be married. Papa allowed Calvin to have her and let him leave the house unscathed. Rev. Simmons supported a forced marriage, and that was their saving grace.

With no help from my great-grandparents, Mom and Dad pulled together a wedding at the community center in the housing projects. Mom was a high school graduate one day, literally blushing bride the next. They attended prom on Friday night and married in a modified version of their prom attire on Saturday. Rev Simmons conducted the ceremony. The seventeen- and eighteen-year-old were hitched with no added guidance, counsel, or even so much as a pep talk. The family served homemade sandwiches and cake for the reception, and the new couple were given the gift of being thrown out into the world. There was no honeymoon, no elaborate send-off, just a typical shot-gun wedding for two kids with a baby on the way. They didn't have a place of their own, so Mom and Dad moved in with Bonnie and her boyfriend after the ceremony. Calvin spent most of the night bent over the toilet from all the alcohol he had consumed. Mom slept in her dress and spent her wedding night alone, crying into her pillow.

The next morning while Calvin was nursing a hangover, Mom heard a horn blowing outside. It was May and Papa. Mom was excited to see them, *Maybe they've come to bring us a wedding gift. Money, I hope!* She anxiously walked outside over to the passenger door where May was sitting and greeted them with a smile. "Hey, mama," she said, waiting to see what the surprise visit was about. It was, after all, the morning after her wedding. But May didn't speak and continued to look straight ahead. Papa turned his eyes toward Mom. He had one hand holding the steering wheel and the other balled into a fist resting on his lap,

"Linda, you get in here so we can go make groceries," May didn't say anything. She briefly glanced at Mom before handing her the list out the window. "After you run dese here errands," Papa said, "we'll brang you back."

Mom could feel the acid in her stomach bubble in her throat. It took all her strength not to let her frustration show. "Yes, sir. Let me get my bag. I'll be right back," she said while retreating to the house. Mom was married with a child on the way and still was expected to maintain her duties at May and Papa's house. She had no choice in the matter. She went over daily to cook, clean, do laundry, and run errands.

Rev Simmons eventually bought Mom and Dad a mobile home of their own. Papa insisted it be placed next door on his land. This made Mom even more accessible to him. He was able to keep a closer eye on her. Mom eventually gave birth to my brother and named him Calvin Jr. I came along thirteen months later.

Mom stayed home as long as she could to care for Junior and me, but the reality of parenting, bills, and responsibilities set in, forcing her to look for work. My father, however, was known not to hold down a job. He was too busy partying at night and sleeping it off during the day, and he also started having run-ins with the law. One day he was shoplifting, and another day he was selling Mary Jane. He wrote hot checks, pressured his friends into petty crimes, and each time he was caught, Rev Simmons talked to the local officials and got Dad off the hook. But all of this took a toll on my mother.

Mom was always concerned that Daddy's actions would land them both in jail. She was reaching her breaking point between his senseless criminal activity and rumors of him cheating with other women around town. Maybe it was feelings of entitlement, the warfare that comes with being a preacher's kid, or the security of knowing Rev would always find a way to fix things, but Calvin took unnecessary risks for a man who had a family. Perhaps he felt trapped by his circumstances, thrust into the role of husband and father, and used alcohol and drugs as a means of escape. Whatever the reasons, his notorious behavior was wearing Mom down.

Mom finally found a job at the bank and lost it just as quickly when Dad took the manager's car for a joy ride and crashed it into a tree. My dad, well, he just called Rev Simmons. Rev paid for the car, but the bank manager fired my mom, and she was never allowed to work there again. Calvin, Sr had ruined her chances at a good job, and she was even more fed up with him. But the ultimate break in my mom and dad's relationship was when my father started doing drugs around us. For the longest time, Dad was able to conceal his drug use from my mom and Papa, who lived next door. He'd close all the windows, pull down the shades, and lock the doors just in case mom came home early or if Papa made a rare impromptu visit.

Mom was starting to catch on to his routine. One day my dad forgot to lock the back door, and when mom eased in, the house was in shambles. She softly walked to the back of the bedroom and found me playing on the floor and my dad smoking marijuana and blowing the smoke into my brother's nostrils. My brother was visibly high; Mom was mortified. Dad, well, he thought it was comical. That is when my mom decided it was time to leave him. Calvin was putting us in harm's way, and that would not be tolerated. Mom walked across the yard to May and Papa's house, and without giving too many details, she humbly asked Papa if we could stay for a while.

Being careful not to activate the nuclear codes, she spoke in a cryptic voice, "Um, Papa, me and Calvin ain't agreeing much and I was wantin' to know if me and the kids can stay with you for a little while." Mom loved my dad and feared Papa might kill Calvin if he knew the details of his infraction.

May, sensing the urgency, nervously chimed in, "Malice, there's no reason why Linda and the chillen can't stay with us. We got plenty room round here." She explained that Mom and Calvin just needed a cooling-off period. After all, they were just two kids raising two kids. But Papa had no sympathy. Instead of allowing her to stay with him, Papa decided to send Mom away to live with her mother Joycelyn, who, by that time, had moved to Washington, D.C. Mom stood motionless and gave Papa a piercing gaze; years of silent thoughts began to amplify in her mind. She snatched the scream that was about to exit her throat and pushed back the tears forming in her eyes. She and her mother were strangers at this point. And after eighteen years of holding her hostage from her own mother and siblings, the almighty one "decided" he was going to send her to live with her family. But she knew what would happen if she dared to challenge him or voice her opinion. So, she said nothing.

Papa never had a conversation with Mom about why he sent her away. He just packed us in the car and gave her a thermos of milk, a wad of money that he instructed her to hide in her shoe, then drove us to the bus station. Mom didn't know how to ride the bus and had never been anywhere on her own. Before boarding, Papa said, "Linda, don't you mess around and drop dat dere thermos. That's all the milk you got for those kids," and those were his parting words. Mom inwardly whimpered as Papa slowly pulled away. With a heavy cloud of uncertainty, as she started up the stairs of the motorcoach, the thermos slipped from her hands and cracked, milk spilled down the aisle of the bus. It was the one thing Papa told her not to do. She stood in the middle of the aisle, frozen, distressed, holding the two of us on her hips. That's when an elderly lady motioned towards her. She put her hand on Mom's elbow, took me in her arms, and whispered, "it's okay dear, do you need help?"

The elderly woman was an angel sent straight from God. She chaperoned Mom most of the way as we traveled northeast. She showed her how to redeem her ticket, what to do at the rest stops, and where to change the luggage. Thanks to her guardian angel, the three of us arrived safe and sound in Washington, D.C. It was a bitter-sweet experience but being booted out into the world with two children only made Mom stronger. At least she was no longer under Papa's rule, and he was too far away to take her children. Mom determined that she alone would raise us, even if that meant it would always be just the three of us. That was our journey to Washington, D.C. That was how and why we were there.

And now we had returned to Texas, with Papa, were it all began.

The Screen Door

Papa was a consistently hard-working man. He still worked at the sawmill. Nothing changed in that regard. He was still strict, not very talkative, and carried that memorable, unique, scent about him. It was a mix between smoldering tar and stale motor oil. I was a teen when I realized it was the smell of snuff. Papa and May dipped snuff, and I was not too fond of it. The smell seemed to permeate through their pores. Snuff is a type of nicotine and apparently addictive. May and Papa would pinch a small bit of brown powder out of a small pocket-sized container and tuck it into the crevices of their bottom lip. It sometimes made their lips bulge like a baboon. That wasn't so bad, but it was the god-awful snuff cans I hated the most. The spit cans were nothing more than a used fourteen-ounce tin container with the lid cut out. It was filled with paper soiled and used to capture the saliva from their mouth. When moisture built up around the snuff, they'd spit the excess saliva in the can. The toilet paper soiled, turned dark brown with saliva. We grew accustomed to seeing and hearing the routine act and sound of spitting. They'd use the same can for several days, and most often, one of us unfortunate souls were responsible for refreshing the can by dumping the saturated paper into the toilet and refilling it again. It wasn't a pleasant experience.

I didn't know growing up that snuff was tobacco. I just assumed it was some medicine that older people needed to help their ailments. Then I concluded it was special dirt that had a unique taste. Why else would they put it in their mouth? On occasion, I'd mimic May and Papa and put a heaping pile of dirt in the bottom of my lip. But it didn't dissolve so easily, and I'd end up having to peel mud out of my mouth. It was hard to clean out, and just when I thought it had all dissolved from my teeth, there'd be a surprise crunch or sandy grit greeting me. At first, it was funny to pretend to dip snuff, but I always regretted it later.

Like clockwork, Papa got up every morning before the crack of dawn to head out to the sawmill. He wore a white shirt, blue jean overalls, and steel toe boots every day. May would be up at three or four o'clock in the morning with her cast iron skillet, grilling slab bacon, over-easy eggs, toast, and making coffee, grits, and pancakes. The smell of breakfast, while delightful, was such a nuisance. As a young girl, I was agitated by the fragrance and sound of cooking. The smoke from the lard, the coffee percolating, the smell of the sizzling bacon were nothing more than an invasion of my senses. The clobbering and clanking of pots and pans disrupted my sleep. It was hard enough to get any sleep at all. I had grown accustomed to the sounds of urban life in Washington, D.C.: sirens, loud voices, the shuffling of cards, and the smell of beer and cigarette smoke. But the nightly serenade of crickets, lizards, flies, cargo trains, and the fan in the window took some getting used to again. Without fail, it seemed, just as I would get into the third realm of a deep sleep, May would taunt my peace with breakfast. It wasn't as if we could get out of bed to hang out in the kitchen and eat with Papa and May before she saw him off to work. No, ma'am, the children didn't fraternize with the adults. We lay in bed until it was time for us to come into the kitchen. Even when it came to simple things like breakfast and dinner, we knew our place and stayed in it.

May was a sweet, gentle soul and a great cook. She was short and plump but well-proportioned for her height and always wore a short bob-shaped wig. I don't know why she never exposed her natural hair, but she'd wear her little synthetic wig until it was adorably tattered. Although she was up before dawn cooking for Papa, May made us a fresh breakfast too. If we couldn't get our taste buds to coordinate, and we all craved something different to eat, May would cook each of us whatever we desired. Mom partly blames May for my brother's lifelong love affair with food. I turned out to be a bit of a foodie myself. I especially loved May's pancakes. They were made in a cast-iron skillet and always crispy around the edges. She'd served them up in thick brown cane syrup or country molasses. The syrup was so thick that it had to be put in hot boiling water to loosen it. Add some slab country bacon, biscuits made from scratch, country ham with a bone in the middle, grits dripping with butter, and we were in hog heaven! It was a regular daily breakfast for us.

No one ever came to the house without eating a little something and catching up on gossip. Everyone in town knew May, and she knew everybody's business. Folks would randomly come through when Papa was at work and sit for a while. May found time to wash clothes on the washboard, hang them on the line, butcher and skin live chickens, clean the house, and tend to the garden. We loved spending days with her; we followed behind her in the yard like little ducklings. Her short height made her easy to cling to and cuddle next to her soft, cotton-like skin. May wasn't intimidating or overpowering; she was sweet, soft-spoken, and loved us dearly.

We felt the same. Every day we looked at her with the same adoration mirrored to us through her endearing eyes.

But May was always worried about something. She had the funniest habit of pacing around the house talking to herself. She'd just ramble on about something or another and expected you to keep up in the conversation as she motioned from room to room. My Mom would often catch the important tidbits and keep the conversation going even though she couldn't hear what May was saying half the time. As kids, we quickly caught on to the technique and just let her mumble her way through the day. I think the constant talking and walking was her way of coping through life.

When we were with May, we were never allowed to leave the yard. I could only go to Ms. Cloudy's house. Ms. Cloudy was an older lady who pressed all the kid's hair. I'd gleefully skip down the road when it was time to get my hair done because Ms. Cloudy always gave a treat at the end. One by one, the girls in town waited patiently to convert kinky, nappy hair to straight and silky. The process of straightening thick, coarse hair was no easy feat and not for the faint at heart.

First, Ms. Cloudy would part the hair and thoroughly saturate it with thick blue grease. The comb, made of iron or some metal, rested on top of the fiery burner to never lose its heat. It usually had a rubber handle. Then Ms. Cloudy would take a small hand towel, wrap it around the handle, and with great precision, pinch the hair at the root with her fingers. With the steady hand of a surgeon, she'd quickly rake the hot comb from the roots through to the end of the follicles. The steam from the comb and oil would blanket the scalp. But no matter how hot it seemed; the only objective was to remain completely still. She was the hair physician, you were the patient, and your

hair was getting fixed. The slightest flinch during the proce-
dure could cause the metal comb to tap the forehead, neck,
ear, or anywhere around the edges of the hairline. And there
was no anesthesia strong enough to relieve the pain of a burn
from a hot comb. It felt like the sting of an angry wasp or
vicious yellow jacket and lingered for days. So, you dare not
move. To move meant that you'd be burned and left with a
bubbling blister or welp, the unspoken symbol of the one who
had moved.

With each stroke, smoke filled the kitchen, and even
with the smell of singed hair and the sound of crackling oil,
there was a joyful feeling of the anticipated outcome, smooth
permed-like hair. At the end of it all, for my bravery and coop-
eration. Ms. Cloudy would give me a cool cup. It was nothing
more than extra sweet Kool-Aid, frozen in a Styrofoam cup.
Still, it was like winning gold at the end of the torment and an
incredibly refreshing reward for being a model patient. I loved
cool cups. I'd lick the layer of thick syrup that had settled on
the top and peel back the Styrofoam as the ice melted down
and got lower and lower. It was a simple but enjoyable treat,
especially on hot summer days.

For the most part, we quickly grew accustomed to the
Texas heat. No matter how hot it was, Junior and I found our
way outside. We played in the front yard because the backyard
was filled with chickens, a vegetable garden, and slop buckets.
Sometimes a couple of kids would come to play with us. On a
particular day, while Mom, Papa, and Junior were at the store,
a girl named Alice came to the yard. She said she was bored
and asked if I would play house with her. Alice was a little
older than me but liked to come to play from time to time. She
was light-skinned, with sandy brown hair, and physically more

developed than most girls in town. "You the mama, and I will be the daddy," she said.

I happily complied. "This is going to be fun!" I thought. I knew what mommas did, so I jumped right into the role. I immediately started cooking and cleaning. We had a pear tree in the front yard. The branches slouched over the clothesline and served as a divider between our land and the neighbors. I yanked four unripe pears from the limbs and pretended to cook. I gathered leaves as plates, set up an imaginary dinner table, and placed them on top of a square tan and brown cobblestone in the front of the yard. Alice was kneeling in the grass pretending to be at work. "Dinner is ready," I announced. We laughed, ate the bitter pears, and pretended to clean the kitchen by washing the leaves in classic kid fashion.

"It's time to go to bed now," Alice said. She instructed me to go to the back of the house by the slop buckets and wait for her with my eyes closed. I did just that.

I could hear Alice tipping around the corner, alongside the back of the house. "She's so silly," I giggled.

"Shh," she whispered, "keep your eyes closed because you are supposed to be asleep." I was even more determined to contain my laughter. I wasn't going to let her spoil my performance. *I'll show her.* I stood still and closed my eyes even tighter. Then there was a strange silence. I was starting to feel a little nervous because I thought Alice would poke me with a stick or something. *What is she doing?* I pondered. Before I could complete the thought in my head, I felt the sudden suction of air without warning.

I grab my guitar. I'm playing it loud,
The strings of the metal will cover the sound.
I know where I am there's nothing to see...

There was a back door with a screen that led straight into the kitchen. May must have walked into the kitchen and seen what Alice was doing to me. The screen door flew open. May busted out of the door with a broom and started screaming, "You leave her be and don't you never come back here again!" May wielded the broom like Babe Ruth aimed to make a home run. Alice scampered across the yard and then took off running down the street. "Don't you ever come back!" May continued yelling. Although we'd see her around town from time to time, Alice never came to play with me again. I couldn't understand what Alice was thinking. I was once again confused. I felt betrayed by her friendship, angry.

I was also frightened of something in me that made people do bad things to me. In my mind, I brought out the worst in Uncle Hunter, now Alice. I thought maybe I was cursed. May's reaction was apparent. Something was terribly wrong. It didn't compute to me that Alice was probably doing something that she had seen someone else do, or worse, what had been done to her. Alice reignited resentment towards my uncle and was another reminder that I was unprotected. Feelings of helplessness and fear seeped into the cave of my mind like the slow drip of a leaking faucet. Once again, someone older than me, bigger than me, had taken from me without my permission. They had taken something they thought was their right to have. Helplessness and fear took root in my mind. Nothing was right or normal, but I had nothing to compare *normal* to, only the familiar rush of rage, anger, and confusion.

May had come to my rescue. If she hadn't caught Alice, I don't know if I would have had the courage to tell anyone. I certainly would have thought her peculiar and lewd behavior was normal. Thankfully, May was there to see the infraction for herself. Something terrible had happened to me, and I was relieved that she knew about it and was going to get some protection for me. May was still fuming when she demanded that I come into the house. *Is she mad at me?* I crouched up the wooden steps, wondering if I would get a whipping from my mom, or worse, from Papa. I inched slowly over to the suede burgundy couch, slouched down into the cushion, and didn't speak a word. May paced the floor talking to herself like she does, especially when worried. To my surprise, she didn't say anything to me directly, never asked me any questions, and never told Mom or Papa what happened. It was as if nothing had happened at all. I learned and accepted that silence, not exposure, was the correct response to these types of incidences. So, I added another layer of armor over my already hardening heart.

Peas and Carrots

After living with May and Papa for a while, we moved to Houston to live with our grandparents, my mother's father Ben, and his wife, Pearl. Mom wanted to be in the city with more job opportunities and better school options. I don't know how my mom reconnected with her dad because she did not have a relationship with him. They had been estranged since she was a child. She never called him *Dad* and always referred to him as the man who abandoned her. I sometimes think about the strength it took to look her father in the eyes after so many years. Not only did Mom have to face the inner conflicts and unanswered questions she harbored towards her father, but being back in Houston meant that my brother and I would see our dad more often. Since he was her first love, reengaging with him for our sakes required an extraordinary amount of courage too.

Grandpa Ben was strikingly handsome with perfect white teeth, bow-legged, with salt and pepper hair. He was an Airforce vet, but he vowed never to fly again due to a rocky flight during Vietnam, described as a near-death experience. Grandpa Ben was the new rock of the family, a new father figure, and stable. He worked for a grocery supply chain and taught us work ethic, how to save, and care for the things we were blessed with. "I don't care if it's just one dollar a day, when you get a job, make sure you always save some money, it'll add up, and you'll always have money when you need it." Grandpa was conscientious, always one for wholesome advice.

"Keep your car clean," he would say. "Take your clothes to the cleaners, they'll keep longer." He was a respectable good man, but he still had flaws. He was a heavy drinker and smoker, stubborn as a mule. But he looked after Junior and me and in many respects, was attempting to make amends for not being the father my mother needed, for not fighting harder to stay in her life. And he'd tell us how he loved Grandmother Joycelyn, but Papa just wouldn't give them a chance.

Grandma Pearl was the polar opposite of Grandpa Ben after she became a born-again believer, but before her conversion, she was a cussing, fussing, drinking, dancing, very loud, boisterous woman. She was known as a domineering fox because she was tall, had a figure like Diana Ross, and was fair skinned with flowy curly hair. She was a chain smoker and dressed skimpily at times to show her smooth, slender legs. But all that changed when she accepted Christ. She went from one extreme to the other. She started wearing long, nearly ankle-length skirts and dresses, no pants, ever, except for the occasional culottes she'd wear when we went fishing. She was still a loud, fast-talking woman but otherwise practically a nun. Her change from foxy party woman to sanctimonious church lady took a toll on her relationship with Grandpa. In fact, it took over a decade for him to see the light himself and start going to church with her. He was resentful that she had brought such a drastic change to their lifestyle. Grandma stopped smoking and drinking cold turkey, and she also stopped listening to what the church called worldly music. She was different outwardly but still feisty and gave Grandpa an unfortunate cursing every once in a while, which he usually deserved, but it didn't help her case for him to know Christ. She was constantly hounding him and pointing out the behaviors that needed changing, which made him even more resistant. Over time, she grew less pushy and concentrated on serving the Lord and finding her purpose in life, with or without Grandpa's participation. After diligently praying for ten years, Grandpa got born again. Not only did he accept Christ, but he became a deacon, a Sunday school teacher, and a regular churchgoer. It was miraculous.

Seeing Grandma Pearl's initial change got me to wonder more about God. She carried on religiously about his goodness and how he had plans for our life. Goodness? Plans? Yeah, right. It was too late for me to receive any goodness from God. I was already ruined. I wasn't about to subject myself to a Holy God because that God let bad things happen to me. God put me in a broken family. God took my purity and innocence. I wanted no part of God's plan. Yet, there was a small drop of curiosity that I couldn't ignore. It gnawed at me. I started to think, *now that you mention it, why am I here?*

Things were getting a bit stressful for my mom living with my grandparents. Grandma was a straight-up "holy roller," which meant we were in another strict environment. We couldn't watch movies, we couldn't eat if Grandma was fasting, we couldn't sleep if she were praying, and we certainly couldn't listen to music. If Grandma Pearl was on an extended fast, even the poor dogs couldn't have food unless the Lord moved on my grandma's heart to give them a little something to eat. Needless to say, Mom started looking for a new job and a new place to live.

Finally, my mom got a job working for the county and found a small apartment in Houston, not far from my grandparents and conveniently located near our elementary school. My mom was working long hours, so my brother and I used to walk home alone after school. I loved walking home with my brother. We were like two peas in a pod, picking up rocks, racing, seeing who could run the fastest, and sometimes we made pit stops on the way. We'd sneak into a club or restaurant and get a few of the mint chocolates from the receptionist stand and dash out the door. My brother and I were latchkey kids, so my mom put the fear of God in us to never open the door for anyone, "not even Jesus," she would say. "I don't care if the Lord himself says he's at the door. You'd better not open it!"

One day Grandmother Joycelyn came by the apartment, but we refused to let her in because we didn't want to get in trouble with Mom. We were too young to realize at the time that it was strange for her to even be in Houston because she still lived in Washington, D.C. But we didn't care! There was no way we were going to open that door!

The apartment was our safe haven. Junior and I were locked in, which meant the rest of the world was locked out. We played jacks on the kitchen floor, ate the afternoon snack that Mom left for us in the fridge, and fiddled around until she came home. We knew when Mom got home all the fun was going to be shut down. I wouldn't say my mom was intentionally mean, but she was strict and no-nonsense like Papa. In hindsight, I can see that she was stressed and sometimes unhappy. After all, she was raising stair-steppers, as they called us. We are thirteen months apart. It felt like we were twins. It was a lot for a young mother with no help. My brother was active and hyper, and I was stubborn. My mom felt she had to be firm because she didn't want us to get out of hand. But I feel she often went overboard in her discipline. There was little room for error. Being a kid was like volunteering to stand in front of a firing squad, always guilty before proven innocent.

On the one hand, we were supposed to be learning about life, and on the other, we should automatically know right from wrong. It was utterly confusing and seemed unfair at times, but that was my mom's universal consensus of parenting. Raising us right and proper meant being overly strict and affectionately getting the taste slapped out of our mouth if ever we dared talk back. It's how my great-grandfather Malice raised her, and naturally, Mom replicated some of those beliefs. Mom was no-nonsense, sometimes mean, always strict, just like Papa.

Once I had a standoff with Mom over peas and carrots. I hated them! And to this day, the smell of cooked peas and carrots together makes me nauseous. My mom made peas and carrots often enough for me to feel tormented, and one time I refused to eat them. We had no choice or input about the food on our plates. We ate what was in front of us, or we got a whipping, plain and simple. But this time, I wasn't giving in. I was willing to take the whipping. It was a risk worth taking. The only problem was Mom didn't care what she spanked us with: a belt, shoe, or the all-parent-loving, child-terrifying switch from a tree. The switch was the worst because it felt like a razor blade slicing over the skin. There was no escaping the aftermath of the sting and welts that lasted for days. Now here I was testing fate and refusing to eat the food she placed before me.

I didn't set out to disobey my mother or make her angry. But all disobedience was a sign of tyranny, and tyranny meant war! There was no room for expressing myself, pleading my case, or trying to explain how I felt. The peas were okay, but the cooked carrots just naturally didn't agree with me. "Eat those peas and carrots, or I'm going to whip you, and I mean it," she demanded, laying out the battle plan and rules of engagement.

"I don't like them," I whimpered.

"I don't care what you like! Eat them before I beat your behind."

But I wasn't giving in. I physically couldn't. I scooped up a spoonful of the peas and carrots, and once the pungent smell hit my nose, I dropped them back onto my plate. I tried again with my fingers pinched over my nose. Still, once they hit my mouth, I had to let go of my nose so I could breathe. I tried to get them down but gagged and spit them out. Then Mom dared me to throw up.

"I wish you would. I don't care how long it takes. You're going to sit there until you eat everything on your plate," Mom said. It was a no-win situation.

This time, I tried again, took another spoonful, chewed them quickly, swallowed, and was still gagging but more hopeful, confident I'd get all of them down. Then "hurgh, hurgh," my stomach spasmed. To my horror, the peas and carrots were fighting back. Within seconds I was holding regurgitated peas and carrots in my hands, saliva dripping between my fingers. I stapled my hands to my mouth, holding on for dear life. Mom's face turned red. She stormed into the bedroom, came back with a leather belt, and slammed it onto the table. At least it wasn't a switch. Then she eased back into her chair across from me and gave me the death stare.

Mom's silence was the calm before the storm. It meant her wrath was brewing, gaining strength. She was unpredictable when she was in that state. The belt was on the table, but she was known for giving an unpredictable whack or sometimes a snatch by the collar. So, I rationalized that the sour stench of the vegetables and stomach bile in my hands was cruddy but bearable enough to avoid a whipping. Fearing Mom was going to knock me out of my chair, I slurped the remains back into my mouth, swallowing the peas and carrots whole, ending the standoff. An hour later, I was sobbing, praying but continuing to swallow them in one gulp, between each whimper, until they were gone.

As I got older, I realized that it was the cooked carrots I hated so much. I liked peas, but the peas and carrots combined made my stomach turn. The smell of cooked carrots makes me want to hurl to this very day. I'm repulsed by it. But I think about how much time could have been saved if my mom had just tried to understand the real issue. I wasn't trying to challenge her authority. It was the carrots. It seems simple, but this pattern of benign neglect, ignoring the symptoms, or the demand to "shut up and do as I say" played out too often. It's the reason why she never got to the root of my pain when I was obstinate and angry. She never bothered to see that many times my acting out or blatant disobedience was a cry for help. I was trying to say I like peas, but I can't stomach the carrots. They make me sick. I can't control or deal with what's happening to me when they infiltrate my body.

I love my mom, and I know she did the best she could, but so many years of unnecessary battles and fights could have been avoided with a conversation. Much like all parents, my mother came with her own set of trauma and battle scars, generational curses. She gave birth to my brother at eighteen years old and was nineteen when she had me. My brother was conceived in teenage love and passion. He was peas! But as for me, well, I was an unplanned pregnancy. She was sick with me at the onset and went to the doctor when her stomach aches were unbearable. The doctor broke the news to her that she was pregnant again. She recalls having a range of emotions. None of them were overtly bad but not necessarily positive either. She said she was speechless, felt unprepared for a second child, frantic even. And because she and my father separated not many years after I was born, the enemy of my mind told me that she resented having me. Something I believed most of my childhood was that I was carrots. I felt like I was force-fed to her, that she only kept me because she had no choice in the matter. I was a big heaping spoonful of warm mushy carrots. Yuck!

Where is Daddy?

We were in middle school when we left the apartment and moved to a trailer park. My brother and I attended three different middle schools in three years. The mobility made it hard for me to focus, plus I kept remembering what my uncle and Alice did to me. By this time, the trauma of molestation had cemented into my brain. It contaminated my thoughts and took over my psyche. I was starting to have memory blocks. The emotions and anxiety I felt were something I couldn't control. My brain would decide what to keep and what to discard. My feelings were always on edge, and I quickly developed a ball of anger that felt like heat resting in the center of my chest or breathing underwater. Middle school was such a blur. Half the time, I couldn't remember any of my teachers, names of friends, or classmates. I couldn't even remember the names of my middle schools.

Oddly, I never forgot to have breakfast. My mom was working a lot, and we no longer had the luxury of May's breakfast buffet. Mom only served us hot sticky oatmeal every day topped with butter, sugar, and canned milk. It was hearty, but we were so tired of having it and looked forward to some variety at school. The breakfast waffles with three mini sausages were my favorite. It came with syrup and a little cup of apple juice. All the other kids seem to enjoy it too. During this time, I started to notice that certain scents and sounds initiated a flood of emotions. The smell of carrots, tomato soup, spaghetti sauce, and ravioli from the can unknowingly put me in an emotional place of anxiety, extreme sadness, or anger. What my mind was shutting out, my senses were taking in, and, when triggered, my heart would pound, and I'd get light-headed, short of breath, and sometimes lose time.

Thankfully Junior and I were visiting Dad more often on weekends and during school breaks. I always felt at ease when I was with Daddy. I loved him very much, and anytime with him was better than no time at all. But periodically, I noticed subtle hints of disappointment and resentment emerging. Resentment takes on an awkward appearance. It disguises like a chameleon and transforms into different shades of expression depending on the circumstance. It's one of those sentiments that's buried so deep that it can fester underneath the surface. The unsuspecting surge of deep resentment often manifested with venom towards others, especially when I was not with him. I didn't like having him part-time. I hated constantly readjusting to my surroundings when I was with him and readjusting again when I returned home. My thoughts were always split between two places, trying to cope without him and wondering what he was doing without me.

During my middle school years, my grandma convinced Mom to go to church regularly, and it wasn't long after that she too became a holy roller. Mom worked long hours, but she spent every free moment she had in church. That's where she met her next husband. Like us, Mom wanted to be loved and wanted a family. But once she started dating, my dad was distant again. Maybe he wanted to give her some space, but I'm the one who felt his long absences. So, I began to look forward to summers when we could stay with him for a week or two.

Spending summer weeks with him was great because it made up for the lost time. One summer, we went to spend time with Dad, and as usual, my brother chose to stay with my Aunt Mattie. Aunt Mattie was my father's sister, and my brother preferred to stay with her and her son Tim because Tim was an only child. He and Junior were more like brothers than cousins. Aunt Mattie lived in a big, beautiful house that sat on several acres of land. While Junior was across town living it up and sleeping in the lap of luxury, I was planted wherever Dad decided to lay his head and subsequently leave me. Dad stayed with whoever he was dating at the time. Most of his girlfriends were unstable. We might be in a cluttered apartment or some drug addict's smoke-filled house. But Daddy had gotten his own place, and we were in his own crummy half-furnished mobile home this time. But that didn't matter to me. It was more important for me to prove that I loved my dad, which meant being with him wherever he was. I was relieved when my dad got a place of his own. At least we didn't have to bounce around. I never wanted to leave his side. His presence alone, the sound of his voice, a gentle hug from him made all the difference in my world. His laugh was contagious, his smile infectious. I needed that. I needed him.

It didn't matter where my dad was going or what he was doing. I was happy to be by his side. Most of the time, he'd drive and roam around here or there, talking and shooting the breeze with people, introducing me as his baby girl. I always felt so proud. He would drive and talk, and I would laugh at his silly way of explaining things. It was the best of times for me, just being with him was more than enough.

Dad had a little two-bedroom trailer tucked on a piece of land between a ranch house and a corner store. I was excited to have a week with him. Junior was with Aunt Mattie, and Dad wanted to make sure I had someone to play with while I was visiting, so he picked up my cousin Trina to stay with us too. Trina was just two years old. It was nice to have some company, plus I felt more mature with her because I was in charge of taking care of her.

Across from my dad's trailer lived a teenage boy named Charles. Everyone called him "Curly" because he was light-skinned with short bouncy curly hair. I thought Charles was the cutest boy I had ever seen, and he seemed to be infatuated with me. I didn't think much of it, though. It was pretty typical. After all, I was from "the big city" of Houston, and the town Dad lived in was small. There weren't a whole lot of girls in the area.

Each time I was there for the summer, Charles and I would meet in the middle of the street to play and have the usual awkward adolescent conversations, discussing typical things kids talk about when crushing on each other. But things turned dark between us. Dad had gone on a drug binge with one of his girlfriends and never returned. He left Trina and me alone for several days. I wasn't too scared on the first night, but we sure did get hungry. Trina was crying, my stomach was growling, and we only had a half loaf of bread. I scavenged the kitchen to see if there was anything edible and found some syrup and ketchup in the mostly bare cabinets. I instantly envisioned a meal. When we were little, my brother and I learned a thing or two about eating and being creative when food ran low. Sometimes we were too hungry to wait for Mom to come home to eat, and one day we discovered yummy ketchup sandwiches.

"Ahh, look at this Trina, we're going to have dinner," I said using a baby voice, trying to comfort and entertain her all at the same time. I took two slices of bread and drenched each side in ketchup, then smashed the two slices together. I slowly tore the sandwich in half, trying my best to make sure Trina's piece was larger than mine. As I handed her the red and white bread to eat, she looked uncertain and hesitant. I continued to put her at ease by biting into the bread, swirling it around in my mouth, and pretending it was a McDonald's cheeseburger.

"Yum, this McDonald's cheeseburger is good," I said with wide eyes and an exaggerated voice. "I'm so glad they didn't put onions on mine," I continued the charade as I crammed the bread into my mouth. Trina giggled and slowly began to eat too. We finished off the ketchup sandwich, and for good measure, I made an identical one with syrup for dessert. Then I took one of three pull-ups Trina had left, changed her, and rocked her to sleep. We staved off hunger and made it through the night.

I was starting to worry when Daddy didn't come back for us. I was more concerned about my father's safety than I was for my little cousin and me. I didn't want my dad to get in trouble if someone found out he hadn't come home and left us there unsupervised. I wasn't going to tell anyone. But the next day, we were playing outside, and the air conditioner in the window stopped blowing. The electricity went out, and I panicked a little. Charles was in our yard tossing rocks, so I rushed over to him and said, "I don't think our lights are on."

"Where's your Daddy?" he asked.

"I don't know, but I know he'll be back soon," I intentionally replied with confidence. "They'll probably come back on in a few minutes, I wouldn't worry about it too much." We went on playing hide and seek and other made-up games. Then I turned on the water hose so Trina and I could drink and keep cool. Charles decided to go into the house for a snack.

"Y'all hungry, want something to eat?" I thought he was going to invite us to his house.

I replied with my head down while rubbing the ball of my foot in the dirt, "Yeah, we hungry." I said, feeling a little embarrassed.

"Just go to Mr. Brown, he'll let you take some food, and your daddy can pay 'em when he gets back."

He was right! Mr. Brown was known for letting folks take a few things and pay later in the week. *Yes, Daddy will be glad to know that I took care of us while he was gone, and he'll see that I'm a big girl.* I grabbed Trina's tiny hand and walked over to the corner store. The bell hanging over the door rang as I pushed it open. I shyly walked up to the counter and explained that Dad didn't come home yet, and we needed something to eat. Mr. Brown didn't ask many questions. He just smiled and said, "Y'all got some bread round yonder?"

"Yes, sir," I replied.

"Okay then, take this." Mr. Brown pulled out some thick bologna covered in red tape and a couple of pre-cut cheese slices, rolled it into a sheet of white waxy paper, and placed the meat and cheese into a paper bag along with a small jar of Miracle Whip. "Here you go dear, I'll talk to Calvin when he gets back," he said while also handing me a half-gallon of sweet tea. Relieved to have food, we hurried back to the house and had seemingly the best bologna sandwiches on earth. The flavor of the bologna, salty cheese, and sweet mayonnaise was divine.

When a child is groomed in an environment of neglect, extreme lack, or violence, it's all normal until there's something else to compare it to. My father and mother were probably poor by most standards, but we didn't know it. Without the exposure to something different or better, it all seemed okay. It was hard to consider in my mind that my father abandoned my cousin and me in a trailer with no electricity. I had no fundamental understanding that it was grossly negligent and irresponsible and possibly dangerous to leave us there alone.

By the next evening, Dad still hadn't returned. So, I put Trina in the bedroom, cracked the windows, and laid on the couch in the living room. I was grateful for the cool breeze. I was just about to fall asleep when I heard a tapping at the door. I knew it wasn't my father because it sounded like a secret knock, as if someone wanted to be heard, but not. I listened to the tap again. It was as if the person was using morse code. I peeled back the sheet covering the window to get a glance. It was Charles. I got up from the couch, walked to the front of the trailer, and gently cracked the door, being careful not to wake Trina.

"Yo daddy home?" he said in a faint voice.

"No, he ain't here. He hasn't come back yet." I was blushing because he was cute, and he had snuck across the street to see me.

"Can I come in?"

"Okay, sure."

"I can't stay long."

"It's alright, the TV don't work without the lights. You wanna talk?" I was sitting on my hands, gently bouncing up and down, excited to have him there. "What you wanna talk about?"

Nothing in me could predict what would happen next. Charles put his hand over my mouth and pushed my back into the couch. *Oh, God.*

> *I grab my guitar, I play it real loud,*
> *The strings of the metal will cover the sounds.*

I scrunched my eyes shut and held my breath for as long as I could.

> *I know where I am there's nothing to see,*
> *And nothing can damage my soul in the sea.*
> *My soul is an ocean, and I am the waves,*
> *My heart is a rock. My mind is a cave.*

As long as I didn't think about it, as long as I could keep it out of my brain, it wasn't happening. And then it was over. I curled up into a fetal position in the corner of the sofa and stared out the window.

"Hey, see you tomorrow," he said as if he was somehow invited and entitled to violate me. I clung to the couch like an old damp towel. I was left alone, feeling ashamed and sick to my stomach. A few hours must have passed when someone pushed open the front door to the trailer. I hadn't moved since Charles left and was too afraid to look up. I couldn't move. I shivered into the corner of the couch, chin squeezed into my chest, gripping my clothes, hoping to be invisible. I peeked from the corner of my eye and realized it was Charles's older brother. I had seen him around before but didn't know his name. I was sure he had come to apologize for Charles, to see if I was okay. The pressure released from my shoulders. I wiped the tears from my eyes and ran my forearm across my nose. I started to speak but tensed up again when I realized he wasn't there to help. He sauntered, tipping through the hallway as if to ensure that no one was there. Then he pulled out a long silver blade from his jacket. I tried to fight back, but he pressed the blade against my throat, and I was afraid he would kill me.

> *Nothing can damage my soul in the sea.*
> *My soul is an ocean, and I am the waves,*
> *My heart is a rock. My mind is a cave.*

"Please. No, no, no, no, no...."

> *I grab my guitar. I'm playing it loud.*
> *My heart is a rock. My mind is a cave.*

Before leaving, he looked at me with disdain and said, "Look at what you made me do." I stayed awake for most of the night and dozed off from sheer exhaustion just before daybreak. I was awakened by a tiny, tender little hand patting my cheek. I looked into my cousin's sweet face and pretended like the night before was just a horrible nightmare. Fresh tears welled in my eyes and merged with the crust in my lashes from the night before. My eyes were swollen, my head was pounding, my soul was aching. *Where is Daddy?*

Later that afternoon, Aunt Mattie happened to come to the trailer after work. She had no idea we had been left there alone for several days. Aunt Mattie was the one steady rock of the family on my father's side. She was an accomplished woman who worked in the judicial system and rose through the ranks in her career. Aunt Mattie was the first black police officer in the rural town of Wharton, Texas, and the first black female to be president of the Texas Alcohol Traffic Safety Association. She was an intelligent, sophisticated woman whose presence was felt the moment she entered the room. Her hair was smooth, most often worn in a classic bun, her dark honey-colored skin flawless. And she had the type of smile that was a privilege to have when given.

But Aunt Mattie seemed to rarely smile. She was the serious, responsible one. There was a stoic air she carried about her, and if you didn't know her well, it would be mistaken for arrogance. She was conservative, not arrogant, a humble woman of standards and conviction. Aunt Mattie didn't entertain bottom-feeders. You had to come up to her level. There were no foolish dealings and ignorant misdeeds with her. And as the first black probation officer for adult inmates, she was always stuck between a rock and a hard place when it came to my dad's indiscretions and criminal activity. On more than one occasion, his file would land on her desk, and she'd have to recuse herself from his cases. I knew that when we sat down to talk, there was no way I could hide the facts. She could spot a lie a mile away.

"Ree, where is your Daddy?" she said in a calm, cool voice. Ree is the nickname my brother gave me, short for my middle name, Sheria.

I knew to give a short answer when being interrogated. "I don't know," I was only going to provide her with the basics in an attempt to conceal that Dad had been gone for days and was nowhere to be found.

"Sheria, you don't look well. Are you okay?"

That's when I blurted out, "I think I'm pregnant."

Mom never really talked to us about the birds and the bees, but she always said, "Do not have sex before you're married. It only takes one time to get pregnant." I took that literally and had no reason to believe otherwise. And given what had happened, well, I naturally assumed I was pregnant and told my Aunt Mattie as much. She could tell I was scared and stressed and didn't ask any further questions. I was also physically ill, fragile, nauseous, and bleeding. Aunt Mattie took Junior and me home and told my mom that I could be having a baby but to wait for twenty-eight days before taking me to the doctor.

Thankfully, I wasn't pregnant, and I was grateful. The fact that I wasn't going to have a baby was a tremendous relief. I was still in middle school and years younger than my mom and Joycelyn when they had kids. The mere thought of me being pregnant brought my family and me an abundance of shame. Mom could not, would not, look at me or speak to me for weeks. I didn't have the courage to tell her what really happened. And even if I did, it would expose my father. Mom was visibly stressed and alienated me for months, and we were not allowed to see my father much after that. I felt like cancer metastasizing into everything and everyone that I cared for. I was not only a disappointment but everything she never wanted in a daughter. At least that's what I told myself. That's what the enemy planted in my head. Everything was my fault, and I wanted to leave to take myself out of the equation of her life. By now, I had learned a little about prayer and began secretly pleading with God, "I can't take any more of this, please, help me."

There were many dark moments ahead. I locked myself in my room for days pretending to be ill. Most times, I was just sitting in the window, numb, in a daze. I had no focus, no friends, no one to talk to at school. I was isolated and wanted to be. I was enraged all the time and would get in trouble at school often for talking back to teachers or fighting other students. My constant aggression eventually landed me in in-school suspension. I was taken out of the regular classroom and general activities and placed in a room with other maladjusted kids. It was the real live version of The Breakfast Club. We couldn't talk to each other. We ate alone in the cafeteria and were escorted to the restroom. It was the perfect isolation I longed for. My mind could not handle being around other kids. Laughter made me angry. Playing made me angry. The fact that the world was going on with business as usual made me angry, and I just wanted to cease to exist.

Abandoned

Mom met someone at church, fell in love, and remarried. She was trying to get on with life and poured all her attention into her new Creole husband. Mom truly loved Marcel; Junior and I loved him, too. Marcel talked really fast with a French accent and broken dialect that sometimes sounded like gibberish. He loved spicy food and loved zydeco music. Zydeco included the harmonica, accordion, and spoons hitting the washboard, making a unique sound. It was different from pop music or go-go beats we listened to in Washington, D.C. At least we knew how to move to the beat of congo drums. Zydeco had multiple rhythms mixed together. It sounded like gumbo wrapped in one beat, and Marcel blasted it around the house.

Mom had gotten born again just before she married Marcel, and out of respect for her, he dialed back on playing too much music in the house. He let Mom determine what we listened to. So, our days were filled with the melodic sounds of Sandi Patty, Amy Grant, Tramaine Hawkins, and locals like Yolanda Adams. Unfortunately, neither artist played the electric guitar, but I liked the Christian music anyway. It was soothing and occasionally moved me in ways I could not explain. There was something about the lyrics, the stories of a Savior. He gave liberty and redemption from sin. The lyrics spoke of His goodness, loving-kindness, and faithfulness toward men. The words often lingered in my head throughout the day and frequently echoed in my sleep. When I found myself getting closer to God, I tried to talk with him from time to time. Most of my talks were about my dad. Or I was vehemently displeased with what He allowed in my life. I never bothered to listen for a reply. I just assumed that God didn't speak back. Plus, I wanted to keep God at a healthy distance because I wasn't sure that He was on my side.

Mom didn't realize it but attending church and listening to Christian music at home shaped my subconscious. Her life-style gave me a different perception of God because I could see that she was becoming a better person. Mom was conservative and reserved before she was saved, and she remained relatively the same after she was born again. The changes in her weren't drastic. She never pretended to catch the Holy Ghost in church or start sounding sanctimonious. The change was in her actions at home, the music she listened to, the places she went (or no longer went), and the servitude she showed a church. Through music, Mom opened my mind about God. Some of the songs included scriptures. Don't get me wrong. She consented to the rules of not wearing pants, shorts, or open-toe shoes. Still, when it came to music, she broke through the Black experience that primarily consisted of what I call spiritual blues with songs like "I'm comin' up, on the rough side of the mountain, I'm doin' my best to make it," I'd hear those types of songs and become even more depressed. But Mom flooded our days and nights with bright, celebratory, uplifting notes from BeBe and CeCe Winans, Carmen, Michael W. Smith, and Rich Mullins. She didn't know it, but just through her music choices alone, I could see that God was not one dimensional, boxed into one way of expression, one way of worship, one sound, one demonstration. She and Grandma Pearl were polar opposites, yet they both remained true to their character to a great extent and faithful to God in their own way.

While I grew to love Christian music, I couldn't resist the urge to rock out to MTV when Mom wasn't home. Junior was playing sports, Mom was working, and my stepfather Marcel was always out and about, I was home alone after school most days. I had the house to myself, and it would be just me, jumping on the bed playing my air guitar to the chaotic sounds of rock and roll. During that time, music videos were relatively new to the world. Instead of watching whatever cartoon was on, an afternoon comedy with Dean Martin and Jerry Lewis, or enjoying sitcoms like *Gimme a Break!*, kids were glued to watching music videos. Instead of just listening to the music on the radio, we could see the artist and whatever imaginative display accompanied their lyrics. Lucifer really upped his game with music videos. He, after all, was the chief musician in heaven, so music is his most powerful weapon. Half the world was hypnotized with the constant streaming of music videos. Before social media, cable TV was the platform shaping the esteem and behavior of kids. Not only did it influence how we dressed, talked, and felt, but it also desensitized us to intimacy, romance, and relationships.

Music kept my mind occupied, and when there was no music I could get lost in, I immediately fell into a state of idleness and questioned my existence. I was so conflicted in my mind that I was dying to talk to someone. I thought one day that I might get the courage to run to my stepfather, who I loved dearly. He called me his baby girl. He seemed to be on the road a lot, but when he was there, it was heaven. His presence was soothing, his voice reassuring. My stepfather Marcel had a way of making me feel like I was the most important girl on earth. He smiled every time he looked at me. I wanted his approval and never wanted to say or do anything to make him dislike me. But I was bleeding emotionally and needed to tell someone about my terrible secrets. I felt like I could trust him. After all, he said he loved me, and he was my father now, I was his baby girl. Marcel said that my brother and I made him proud and that he would never leave us. I tossed the idea back and forth in my mind of confiding in him. Because after what happened at Dad's trailer, I believed I was viewed as a loose, fast girl. He needed to know the truth about what really happened.

Subconsciously, I blamed myself and thought maybe I deserved it. But Marcel was there now, and I knew he would understand, take my side, talk to Mom for me, and help us sort things out. I was definitely going to do it! I was going to tell Marcel everything when I got home. I knew he would protect me. I got off the school bus and hurried to the house, but when I turned the key to open the door, I was in utter shock. I stood in the doorway blinking for a few seconds and did a double-take. Our belongings were gone. The furniture, pictures, and table were gone. I quickly ran to Mom's room and saw that most of her stuff was gone too: the dressers, the clothes in the closet, everything, gone. For a split second, I thought I somehow wandered into the wrong house. I immediately grabbed the phone and called Mom at work.

"Mom."

"Yes, what is it CeCe," she replied. My mother always called me CeCe, even though the rest of my family called me Ree.

I stuttered out the words, "Our stuff is gone."

There was nothing but silence.

"Mom," I said nervously, "the furniture is gone."

More silence. Mom finally replied calmly, seemingly unbothered, "Wait a minute, CeCe."

"Mom, did you hear me? I think someone broke into the house and took our stuff." I was in a panic, demanding that she say something more.

Mom finally spoke again, "Hold on a minute," she sighed, likely trying to find a private place to talk.

I persisted, "Mom, where is everything? Where is Marcel?"

Speaking in a low tone as if pressing her mouth to the phone, she said, "No one took anything, and Marcel is gone."

"What? Gone where?" more silence.

"We'll have to talk about this when I get home," Mom insisted.

"But Mom, where did he go? Is he coming back?" I didn't know if *gone* meant dead or if it meant he was just no longer with us, in our house.

"No, he's not coming back, okay. I have to get back to work. I'll see you when I get home. We'll talk about it then," She hung up the phone.

There is something so traumatic about coming home to an empty house. It's a visual forever etched in my mind because I could see abandonment. Abandonment had become a polaroid, a new emotional keepsake. If, by chance, I should forget what abandonment looked like, all I needed to do was reflect on the instant snapshot stored in my memory. I began a routine habit of chanting inwardly, "My heart is a rock. My mind is a cave. My heart is a rock. My mind is a cave." I had already experienced a form of abandonment with Dad, and now for Marcel to be gone, without warning, it was too much for me to take.

It was as if Marcel had vanished into thin air. I sat on the living room floor where the couch used to be and waited, for what seemed like a lifetime, for Mom to get home. I waited with anticipation for her to pull up to the driveway. When she finally arrived, she walked into the house, into her room, closed the door, and she never talked about Marcel again. Ever. Instead, I was left to wonder. She never explained why he was gone, where he had gone, or if we'd ever see him again. She didn't tell us what happened, and we didn't ask. We learned at an early age not to question her or any adult for that matter. He was gone, and that was that. And it was just the three of us, again.

Marcel and any sense of security I had were gone. There were countless days I sat in my windowsill, hoping he would come back and hoping I would die. Self-loathing was a part of my daily routine as I started mastering the art of internalizing pain. So many days, I sat on that window waiting, hoping he would come back. I wondered why he would leave us, why God would allow this. I decided I didn't need God. I didn't need anyone or anything. I alone would protect myself. I would be my own safeguard. My alter- ego, Sheria was in charge now. She would hold my sanity and assist me in transferring the pain to someone else. I became more hardened, more aggressive, numb, and filled with blind rage. *Where's my Daddy? Where is Marcel? Where's God?* Who cares!

Revival

With Marcel gone, we eventually moved into a small house not far from my grandparents. It was a white house with red concrete steps and an all-red landing on the front porch. The house wasn't far from the Church of God in Christ we attended, the predominant denomination for African Americans in the south. "You can't join in. You've got to be born…" the congregation sang with robust pride every Sunday during morning worship. Mom became even more committed to all things God and dragged us to church every moment she could. She and Grandma Pearl had been drafted into the special forces of holy-rollers.

Mom faithfully served the pastor, who was later elevated to bishop, and he and his wife gravitated to her. The pastor's wife was barren, never able to have kids, and they loved and trusted Mom so much they publicly referred to her as their adopted daughter. They treated her as their own. Not only was she a daughter to them, but she was also an adjutant, driver, secretary, cook, and was always personally taking care of them in any way she could. The only problem was that the bishop had two churches, one in Houston that was within walking distance from our house and another in Liberty, Texas, about an hour outside Houston. Mom would drive the bishop several times a week from Houston to Liberty, with my brother and me, usually fast asleep in the back seat.

Bishop had two Sunday services, sometimes three if there was an afternoon program or evening service. He taught Bible study and had a mid-week service, one day in Houston, another in Liberty. Living so close to the church made it convenient for us to be there all the time. We stayed in the church from Sunday to Sunday: Bible study, volunteer programs, youth choir, Easter and Christmas speeches, revivals, baptisms, pastor anniversary, missions night, women's meetings, choir anniversary, Bible band, watch night service, sunrise service. And when there was no service, we'd be there cleaning or sitting while Mom typed Bishop's sermons. It was church in the morning, church in the evening, all week long, all year long. I used to think, *How much God do we need? Is there a point when we have met our quota? Does God have an off day, like during creation when he rested?* As a family, we never took a day of rest and never took vacations. All we knew was school, church, and whatever trip or activity the church decided to do.

The COGIC church was true to the southern Bible Belt culture: big hats, fine suits, overly extended services, dinners after church, sometimes breakfast before service, hand-clapping, foot-stomping, tongue talking, and praise dancing. Women and girls had to wear pantyhose and girdles and didn't even think about wearing pants in or outside the church. Most things I never questioned, I had no reason to and knew better not to. But I wanted to know why God was so concerned with the dress code. I mean, why did we all have to look alike. I wanted to wear big wild hair and colorful clothes like Cyndi Lauper. From time to time, I was able to get away with a different hairdo but no pants or sandals. As for red nail polish or sleeveless dresses, well, that would have me cast into the eternal lake of fire.

There was much preaching in COGIC about fire, hell, and brimstone. Most teens my age got saved out of fear, especially after seeing the tribulation movie where kids got beheaded if they didn't take the mark of the beast. Getting saved was not an easy feat. We had to work for it. It included two or three nights, usually during a revival, of uttering "save me Lord, save me Lord, save me Lord, save me Lord, save me Lord," until you were foaming from the mouth. Somehow saying it repeatedly demonstrated obedience and sincerity to the people at the altar. They were the ones you had to convince of your spiritual transformation. They called it tarrying. It felt more like torture. I mean, was God deaf and hard of hearing? What was the point? We finally came to realize that unless we put on a good show and managed to squeeze some tears from our eyes, we were never going to get the stamp of approval and confirmation from the missionaries that we were born again or indeed saved.

The missionaries were women who prayed, sometimes taught, and most times dressed in all white. COGIC church didn't believe women could pastor, be an elder, preach, and certainly couldn't stand in the pulpit. Women could only be an evangelist or a missionary, and that was it. The missionaries were serial altar workers, and it didn't matter whether or not you thought God heard your sinner's prayer the first time or if you even sincerely meant it the first time, no approval from them, no salvation for you.

They had to believe that we had *got salvation*, or you left the altar still a sinner and would have to try again another time. Want the Holy Ghost? Come, stand at the altar, and repeat. If we wanted to be filled with the Holy Ghost, it usually had to happen during the next revival or shut-in prayer, unless, of course, we were deemed saved on the first or second night of the meeting. The missionaries kept track of who got saved, who almost got saved, and who needed to be filled with the spirit. Kids didn't get filled with the Holy Ghost at home or just sitting on the pew. No, ma'am, you had to be at church, at the altar, with witnesses. Getting the Holy Ghost was Salvation 2.0 and the next level of scrutiny and evaluation. Even if it meant that service went on till midnight, especially if it was the last night of the revival, we had to speak in tongues before they'd turn us loose. After being summoned to the altar four or five nights in a row, by the last night of the revival, we were determined to get the Holy Ghost. It was time to get to work. We'd hold our arms up seemingly for hours, and after petitioning God one hundred times to "fill me Lord, fill me Lord, fill me Lord," just at the point of reaching muscle failure, we'd just start mumbling in a mad-like fashion: Jee, jee, jezz, zzz, jee jee jee jee. That was usually enough to receive a thumbs up from the women's committee in white after you were dripping beads of sweat and weak in the knees.

As a kid, I sometimes thought church was wild and that some people were nuts! The yelling, dancing, loud music, running, screaming, they were casting out demons, is all I knew. But the demons must have made a few stops on their way out because while the adults were dancing, beating the tambourine, and raising the roof, many of us girls were getting felt up by boys right on the pew. There was kissing in the choir room and all sorts of things happening in cars in the parking lot. The adults were getting Jesus while the kids were testing Jesus. It's horrible to admit, but true. However, church wasn't all doom and gloom.

There were many fun times at church, especially when the youth choir had rehearsal. The energy we had as young people was contagiously electrifying. The church is also where

I formed lifelong friendships with people who became like family, and it's where I met my best friend, Laynette. Laynette was from California and had an entirely different persona and perspective on church and life in general. She had a bright smile, cinnamon brown eyes, perfectly straight teeth, and a bounce and sway in her walk. She wasn't trained to say "no ma'am" and "yes, sir" to everybody like we were, but she spoke properly and was always respectful and kind. Her parents were good people, and since her father was a minister, she was in church sometimes just as often as I was. But Laynette had no intention of being restricted by manufactured religious rules and wouldn't prove anything to anybody. When the rest of us were summoned to the altar, we knew the routine and went right into action, but Laynette would have no part of it. She often just stood there smiling with the altar workers pressing her to "open your mouth and ask God to save you." She may utter it once or twice, but after five minutes or so, she'd quietly exit the crowd, to head back to the pew, with the clear under-standing that she'd be labeled as *NSY: not saved yet*. As far as I was concerned, her bravery and refusal to conform made her a girl with a guitar, which meant eternal friendship in my book.

Laynette's parents, brothers, and cousins became my extended family. We were besties, like sisters, and her family always treated me with open arms. Mom wholeheartedly trusted Laynette's parents and would allow me to have sleepovers with her and her cousins. I looked forward to the sleepovers because that most definitely meant we'd have Laynette's mom's famous homemade three-layer cake and ice-cold milk to wash it down. Our friendship gave me newfound freedom; I had somebody to talk to. She was the sister I didn't have and the partner in crime I needed when it was time to rebel against the world and against religion.

Once during a revival, Laynette and I came to a consensus that we had had enough church. So, while everyone was "caught up to meet him in the air," we slipped the keys out of her Aunt's purse and went for a joy ride. No one was the wiser. We were back in time for the altar call. We were so successful in our first heist, this became the first of several great escapes. We learned how to plan appropriately and get the timing just right. We knew not to be gone too long and to ease out of services only during high tide. We grew even cleverer when the worship services were offsite, especially at the COGIC youth conferences. It was usually held at a hotel or convention center. Most of the activities and breakout sessions were geared toward youth, which meant no parents in our workshops. So instead of going to the actual workshops, we'd make a mad dash for the hotel pool where, undoubtedly, there were one or two other rebels, but not a snitch in sight. We had no fear of getting caught because the adults didn't go to the pool. The saints didn't wear bathing suits, that also landed you in the lake of fire, so that meant they didn't swim either. The pool area was a parent-free zone. We'd enjoy the serenity of the water and then secretly make our way back to the room to shower, wash and dry our hair, and put on the same outfits. Later we'd join the rest of the group in the general session. And when asked what we learned, we'd reply with something along the lines of "it was so much good information, we really can't recapture it all right now," then glance over to each other as if to say, kudos, we did it again.

Those were some of the best times, and we were the best of friends. Whenever I stayed at Laynette's house, I had free reign.

Her brothers were my brothers, her room was my room, and her kitchen was my kitchen. There were no restrictions. I was always treated with love and kindness. We laughed together, cried together, schemed together, tried to figure out God and life together. She was the only person in the world I could be fully transparent with without feeling judged or ridiculed. She knew my secrets too but never viewed me as damaged goods or less of a person. She knew the pain I was experiencing, the war raging in my mind, was acquainted with my alter-ego, Sheria, yet she always saw the good in me. Laynette had her own demons too and life's challenges to face, and maybe that is why we never viewed each other as a burden or a lost cause. She and I made perfect friends because we understood each other.

Laynette had a special relationship with her father, and I understood that too. I liked being around her dad, or rather, I enjoyed being around Laynette with her Dad. He was quite the jokester, and anytime he'd dish out orders or start fussing, he'd direct it toward me too. I liked that about him and her mom. They made me feel like an equal opportunity family member. Her father joked with me just like he did with all his kids and evenly distributed his "what do you girls think you're doing," speeches. I usually let Laynette do all the talking if things got out of hand, I certainly wasn't going to talk back to him. Plus, Laynette's whole objective was to end or win an argument. She would argue back with her dad, almost word for word, all the while with a smile.

From the outside looking in, it might appear that Laynette was disrespectful to her father, but they had a special kind of relationship. They could seemingly talk about anything, and when he'd get upset and start huffing, she knew how to tame the beast.

The arguments were pure entertainment. "Oh, Daddy, you talking louder isn't going to make me agree with you more," Laynette would say with a giggle. Her dad would raise his voice determined not to let her get a word in. Laynette would press even more, "oh now, you want to keep repeating what you said, well okay, that doesn't mean you're right, Daddy," she'd taunt in a gentle, playful tone. "Oh, alright, I'm just going to let you keep saying it if it makes you feel better because I had a point too, Daddy, but you don't want to hear it." I loved the way she called him daddy.

Usually, by this time, I, Laynette, her cousins, who were usually part of the gang, would be laughing so hard that no one could even remember what they were arguing about in the first place. And if the battle didn't end, Laynette's mom, Beatrice, would readily intervene. Fully suited with the proverbial referee's stance, Beatrice would sweetly utter in her ultra-proper voice, "Oh Willie, please, would you all just let it go for now. Isn't there something better to talk about? Laynette, would you both just let it go. Neither one of you is making any sense at this point." Her tone, though gentle, would cause them to go to their neutral corners. Neither would win the argument, but we were all thoroughly entertained.

Incarcerated

My dad started getting into more trouble with the police, and we saw him less and less. I was missing my father so very much and longed to have any communication with him. Every time the phone would ring, I'd pray that it was him. Sometimes it was, most often not. It wasn't a very substantial conversation when we talked, but to me, every word was worth its weight in gold.

"Hi Daddy!"

"Hey, Ree. How you doing, baby?"

"I'm doing okay, where are you?"

"Oh, Daddy is staying with a friend for a little while." That was code for one of his lady friends.

"When can I come and see you? I miss you daddy."

"I'll check with your mother and see when she can bring y'all down."

Daddy never came to get us himself. Either my mom or Aunt Mattie had to do all the driving. It was so inconvenient for them. But he usually didn't send for us anyway. The conversations were short "Well, Ree, Daddy's gotta go. I was just calling to check up on you and your brother. Daddy loves you and will talk to you soon." He never left a conversation without saying those three words.

"I love you too, Daddy," and that was usually the extent of it. He always seemed preoccupied, never fully present. But I gladly accepted what I could get from him.

Although Mom knew about Calvin's run-ins with the law, she never spoke badly about him to us. He was her first love and biggest heartbreak and had every right to be bitter and angry. But she always encouraged us to see him, talk to him, and spend time with him when possible. She never stood in the way as some single mothers intentionally do to keep us from seeing him. It was Calvin's own actions that ultimately tore us apart.

Mom arrived home early one day after school to tell me we would be leaving to pick up Junior from football practice. It was unusual for her to come home early from work, plus Junior always rode home with one of his teammates. There was something strange in her countenance, no particular expression on her face. Mom sat steadfastly behind the steering wheel as she drove to the high school where he was practicing. No music was playing, just the booming sound of nothingness. I gazed out the backseat window, too afraid to ask questions, feeling as if someone with cleats was standing in my chest. I didn't know what happened but knew something had to be wrong because Mom never picked Junior up from practice. When the car pulled up to the field, Junior looked over. I could see the nervous energy in my brother's eyes, the look of anxiety over his face, the question mark swirling in his head. Holding his helmet in hand, he grabbed his duffle bag, looked over his shoulder and gave a nod goodbye to his teammates then walked solemnly towards the car.

Once he was settled in, Mom said, "Your father Calvin is in prison," we were both stunned. "And he's not getting out."

Junior's voice was shaking while he fought back tears. He asked, "For what, what did he do?"

"I don't know, but I think he was given a life sentence."
I suppose Mom said something more, but I couldn't hear
anything else. My mind suddenly went blank, and my ears
were deaf as if swimming underwater. I could only hear the
muffled sound of her voice and feel the pressure in my chest
rising to my head. *Prison?* I knew my dad had been getting
into trouble with the police and had done a short stint in jail
here and there, but prison was permanent. He might as well
have been presumed dead. I was breathless. Junior and I both
sat spellbound on what seemed like a never-ending ride home.
It hit me. I would never see Daddy again, for real this time.

After Mom told us that Dad was in prison, that was the
end of the conversation for her. In typical adult fashion, she
pulled the clip from the grenade, dropped a bomb, and moved
on, not realizing we had just been emotionally maimed. My
mother didn't know anything else to do. She did to my brother
and me what Papa did to her. Looking back, Mom must have
been hurting too.

If only I had forced a conversation, screamed, and cried
in that very moment instead of concealing my hurt and disappointment. Masking the pain of my father's incarceration
had a lingering impact for so many years. My life was already
a mess, and it got worse in an instant. Everything in my world
was suddenly broken beyond repair. I had never felt that kind
of sadness before. The pain was so deep I couldn't absorb it all.
I just wanted to take a long sleep. Sheria always urged me into
a deep sleep when things were too much to process. If only
Mom had reached out to console me with a hug or a touch. But
there was no consolation, nothing, not then, not later, not ever.
We went on with business as usual.

For the next several months, I walked around in a haze. I couldn't think or feel anything. My heart was colder and more numb than it had been before. Even though my dad and mom had long been divorced, he was still my everything. I was his baby girl, his little princess, and he could do no wrong. But when hearing of his incarceration, I immediately felt orphaned, rejected, abandoned again, and there was a new feeling that emerged: unlovable. I had so many questions. My imagination was brutally incessant and took on a life of its own. What had he done that was so terrible that would cause him to be sentenced to thirty-six years in prison? The thought alone single-handedly crippled me. I couldn't bear him being out of reach. From that point onward, I never mentioned my dad again unless some asked, and I stopped calling him Dad but referred to him as Calvin, Sr.

The prison where my father was placed was about an hour-long drive. Junior would go to visit as often as any dependent child could. When he wasn't busy playing football, making the dean's list, and protecting me, he would ask Grandma Pearl or Grandpa Ben to take him to see Calvin, Sr. But I couldn't muster up the strength to go with him at first. His imprisonment enraged me even more, and I was exasperated with grief and hostility.

As I began to connect the dots of my life, it was clear that Calvin was the culprit of every bad deed that happened to me. His absence left me open to being victimized and humiliated. He caused the breakup with my mom, and I got molested. He was doing drugs, and I was raped. He was always out of place, and the predators rushed in time and time again to devour me as unguarded prey. My father was behind bars, and now I was shuffling through life shackled. The heavy, rusty fetters of bitterness and profound regret were dragging me. I was impaired, confined, caged. The welcoming sound of the metal prison bars had slammed and clicked shut. I was locked in unforgiveness.

Having no one to turn to, I started drinking alcohol. I started taking money from my grandparent's secret money jars to buy cheap alcohol on the way to school. That created a domino effect. I was suspended or put in detention regularly for being drunk or for cursing the teachers. I wanted someone or something to take the pain away. I wanted the mysterious God in heaven to come down and save me from my circumstances, but I didn't know how to ask and did not believe that he would answer.

I didn't know how to pray, so I'd mumble a word or two here and there in hopes that God would be eavesdropping. A silent cry. A whisper of desperation under my breath, *Please, God, please make the hurting stop. I can't take anymore. I can't do this.*

Mom was in church so much I started to learn scriptures and a lot about the God of the Bible. Unknowingly, the place that I wanted to avoid was equipping me for the battle of my life. I grew more and more curious about God and His miracles, while at the same time, I wanted to know why He was so hostile towards me. What had I done to deserve his wrath? Why was God mad at me? I wanted answers but, I had ill feelings towards Him. Yet there were times when I could feel that He was near like a gentle breeze on the back of my neck, hovering.

To some degree, Junior and Calvin, Sr. grew their relationship while he was in prison. I couldn't understand how they could be so close when I was the one who stayed with Calvin when we went to spend the weekends or summers with him. I still longed for any love and attention he could provide for me, but he was in prison, with a thirty-six-year sentence. There was nothing he could do for me. Still, I worried about him. I had heard and seen things on television about people in prison and thinking about those things nearly gave me a nervous breakdown. I was taking on the burden of his safety with a million *what-ifs. What if he gets into a fight, what if he's put in solitary, what if he's sexually assaulted, what if he kills himself, what if he dies in prison, what if he starves to death, what if he gets sick, what if the other prisoners kill him. What if? What if? What if?* Nothing good comes from a child carrying the weight of adult problems. No child can emotionally withstand the weightiness of complex life issues. I wasn't mature enough and hadn't lived long enough to navigate the psychological land mines.

As much as I had experienced, I was not prepared for the additional emotional strain of an incarcerated parent. There was no orientation, no class, no course 101, no book entitled *What to Expect When Your Parent is in Prison.* I was expected to go to school and church and continue with life as if nothing had happened. But my heart was heavy all the time. I was manically depressed and lived in a constant state of hopelessness. I carried feelings of guilt as if somehow, I had contributed to or was partly the cause of my Dad's circumstance. I started acting out even more in school: drinking, smoking marijuana, fighting, carrying guns, and acting promiscuously. I had horrible grades and sabotaged every opportunity afforded to me to excel. I put up walls and barriers to keep from being hurt. My mind was confined, and I intentionally kept anyone and anything I thought could hurt me at a distance. "My heart is a rock, my mind is a cave," was my daily anthem.

Mood swings and memory blocks increased dramatically. There were countless moments when I would lose time and not remember what transpired around me or moments when I would hyperventilate and blackout. My alter-ego was fighting to remain in control and often did at times. I wanted to exist, but it was too risky to stay in the reality of my world. It felt better when Sheria was in charge. She allowed me to be a spectator and opt out of life. She determined what to absorb and what to discard from my brain. I hid in plain sight while distancing myself from the rest of the world. My emotions were no longer strained because I didn't have any. I didn't feel at all. I grew cold and calculating and became fixated on learning how to make men hurt the way I had been broken.

Sheria became my protector. No one would tell us what to do, how to act, or what to feel, not even God. She was strong, a fighter, and wasn't afraid of anyone or anything. She challenged authority and did not care about the consequences. What was right or wrong didn't matter as long as I didn't feel anything. I observed the outside world from afar; I was securely detached. But sometimes, in the early morning or in the still of the night, the weight of the God's Spirit would overwhelm me, and I'd find myself sobbing in my bed, quietly groaning in my pillow, gasping for air. My emotions would flood in like a tidal wave, but then peace. I knew it was the Holy Spirit because his peace blanketed me and swaddled me like a newborn baby. Then I would breathe, rest, sleep without nightmares.

Unless triggered by a particular scent or sound, I was in survival mode throughout my entire span of high school. The only absolutes were whatever Sheria conspired and approved. When I could not abide under her protection in an alternate universe, I panicked. Thoughts of death would consume me. I could not fathom a life without the pain, and as far as I was concerned, I was already a walking zombie. I was so furious at God for taking away what I thought my life could be, better yet, for not giving me a fair chance. I had no choice in my purity. I didn't choose my father. I couldn't change who I had become.

But then I'd be in church or hear a televangelist preaching about new life. I was either slightly hopeful or offended by their conviction and belief that God was good and wasn't out to destroy me. How could they know with certainty that God loved me when everything around me was so evil? What kind of God would inflict me with so much pain? Although I had moments of hope, I wasn't spiritually strong enough to withstand the warfare against my mind.

I equated God the Father to Calvin, Sr.—cruel, inconsistent, somewhere *up there* doing whatever he wanted to do, aloof, while I suffered. I had questions and a deep curiosity that I could not shake. I started looking forward to being at church. The lively expressions of worship were a welcome change to my monotonous life. It was like attending a football game for the home team. That meant that I, too, could cheer, yell from time to time, relieve some tension, blow off some steam. But my main objective was to study the scriptures thoroughly enough to disprove God's love towards me. God was on trial.

The more I learned in Sunday School, the more I wanted to know. I was deeply perplexed by the biblical patriots who had gone through terrible circumstances but still chose to serve God. I started reading the Bible at home, privately; I could envision the people and sound of God's voice. The more I read the Word of God, the more I began to understand his character. His essence was becoming more tangible, and the words appeared to lift off the page:

*I have **loved** you with an **everlasting love**; I have drawn you with unfailing kindness.*
Jeremiah 31:3, NIV

*For God so loved the world that he **gave** his one and **only Son**, that whoever believes in him shall not perish but have **eternal life**. For God did not send his Son into the world to condemn the world, but to **save** the world through him.*
John 3:16-17, NIV

*Take my yoke upon you and learn from me, for I am **gentle** and humble in heart, and you will find **rest** for your souls.*
Matthew 11:29, NIV

*If we died with him, we will also **live** with him; if we endure, we will also reign with him. If we disown him, he will also disown us; if we are faithless, he remains **faithful**, for he cannot disown himself.*
2 Timothy 2:11-13, NIV

I found myself obsessing over the letters in red when Jesus was speaking and grappling with the possibility that God's intentions towards me were not all evil. I was expressly interested in why Jesus would give his life for me and how Jesus used his power. I wanted power too. I want the power to rewrite my past and project my future. If Jesus could heal the sick and raise the dead, then maybe, just maybe, he could change my life. Instead of watching music videos, I started listening to the preachers on television, gradually becoming lured into another alternate reality. I studied the Bible with great tenacity to see there was a world where I didn't have to suffer alone, a place where I could dwell in peace. According to the Bible, my life had a purpose. If I was in Jesus, even the unthinkable things that happened to me could somehow work in my best interest. It seemed utterly impossible, but I had the smallest seed of hope that maybe… just maybe… the words were true.

The Lumberjack

My teen years grew increasingly hard, not just for me but for my entire family. Mom constantly left her job to come to the principal's office because I was being reprimanded or suspended. Junior got in trouble for trying to protect me from my misdeeds. The only time he was ever suspended from school was because of me, which blemished his outstanding academic and attendance record. Junior and I had a loving relationship. We are just thirteen months apart and might as well have been twins, but our relationship was strained.

Mom taught him to get dressed, pick out my clothes, and dress me for school when we were little. As teens, he did my hair when Mom was too busy trying to keep food on the table. We were latchkey kids, so we put together our meals, cooked, and did chores together. When it came to homework, he was great in math, and I was great in English, so we'd get our lesson done and swap papers. He would check my math, and I would check his essays. We were responsible in that regard, and unfortunately, he was given a permanent role at the helm of our relationship because he was the oldest.

We did everything together, always in the same grade going through life at the same pace, but somewhere along the way, he was designated to play the role of a parent. By the time we got to high school Junior was trying desperately to be my brother and father simultaneously, a role no boy should feel obligated to fill. He felt compelled and thought it was his responsibility to look after me. While it's an honorable and loving thing to do, it was burdensome because my brother was trying to fill shoes he had never walked in before. Like me, he was likely depressed at times and struggled with his self-esteem. But who did he have to turn to? Who was his counselor or mentor? He was just as much abandoned by Daddy as I was and then faced with the assumption that he was required to fill the void. I could see that he was trying to guide me, but this new role caused tension in our otherwise close-knit siblingship. We became increasingly combative. He started taking a hard stance ordering me around and chastising me. I didn't like it at all and resented him for it. Once Junior caught me smoking a cigarette and threatened me within an inch of my life. Then he heard that my boyfriend had pushed me, so Junior stormed into the school and beat the poor boy, no questions asked, and threatened to kill him. The more he tried to control me, the more it made my blood boil.

He took his role as the self-appointed man of the house seriously and was just as protective of mom as he was of me. If he perceived that someone was thinking about getting aggressive with mom or heard someone speak to her in a disrespectful manner, he went off the rails. I will never forget when we were in the church cafeteria when this lady said something mean to Mom. This particular lady didn't like Mom, for whatever reason. Before we could fully hear what was said, Junior lunged at the poor lady! His temper was on steroids. Tables and chairs went flying. Multiple people had to physically restrain him. It was an awful scene.

Our father, Calvin Sr., should have been there for both of us. Junior needed him just as much as I did. Junior had to learn to grow to be a man while pretending to be a man. He was overseeing my emotional well-being while neglecting his own unchecked emotions. Every once in a while, when we had blinders on and convinced ourselves that Calvin's absence was not affecting his namesake, Junior would explode from a dark place so deep that we feared he would destroy his own life and wind up in a cell next to Daddy. Thank God that never happened, but there were so many intimate moments when it almost did. His temper nearly destroyed him.

I appreciated my brother's protection, but I did not want him acting as if he was my father. I just wanted my brother, my friend. One day at school, we got into an argument. I don't even remember what we argued about. But I yelled at him to the top of my lungs, "I hate you! I don't need you! I hate you" I could see that my words cut him deeply. I didn't hate him. I hated Calvin, Sr., and well, Junior was the boy, the imposter, who was wearing his shoes.

The role young boys are forced into due to an absentee father is daunting. It's like being a lumberjack. The work of a lumberjack has to be one of the most dangerous jobs there is. These men are responsible for harvesting and removing trees that stand hundreds of feet tall. The process of cutting down the tree is the hardest because if not cut in the right place, the tree could fall in the wrong direction and inadvertently kill other trees, or worse, the lumberjack himself. If cut correctly, well, that's a good thing, but it still has to be pruned, hauled, and transported. You need the right equipment to pick up the massive trunks, pull them out of the middle of the forest, and take them to a place where they can be put to good use. It's tedious and dangerous work even for a veteran lumberjack, and they are always at risk of physically injuring themselves. I imagine that is what fatherhood is like.

Even the best fathers find it challenging to raise a child. Yet, countless boys are forced into fatherhood every day, children trying to raise children. As with me, Daddy wasn't there for major events or accomplishments in Junior's life. Junior did not see Daddy shouting from the stands at the football games, cheering in the crowd alongside other fathers. He was not there sitting in the audience, beaming with pride when he received awards for academics. Dad wasn't there for him to consult when it came to his first date, his choice in girls, his career, or to guide him when he had significant concerns about life. My brother didn't have a father, just like I didn't have a father, and he needed him just as much as I needed him.

Later that evening, Junior sat next to my mom and said, "Mama, I can't do it anymore. I can't look after Ree. I just can't do it. She won't listen to me and now I'm getting in trouble in school because of her." He sounded like a man who had just put down his best friend, a wounded dog. Except he was no man at all, he was just a kid like me who was dealt an unfair hand and carried the weight of it all. The lumberjack was yelling "timber," the clarion call to let everyone within hearing distance get out of the way because I was being cut down.

I was sniffling in the background when I heard Junior's words to Mom. Once again, I was starting trouble, and I decided it was time for me to leave. I wrote a long farewell letter to my mom the next day and ran away from home. I placed the sealed envelope on the table, bolted out the front door, and ran as fast as I could in the direction of the church. Pumping my arms with every stride, I ran, stumbling and zig-zagging, trying to breathe and soothe my burning lungs. Once I ran out of steam and the adrenaline began to fade, I realized I had no place to go, nowhere to turn. I wanted to do everyone a favor by vanishing, but I had no money, no nearby friends or relatives, no plan.

When Mom found the letter, she sent Junior to look for me. He found me sitting like a lost puppy on the church steps, sobbing. I looked up, and there my brother was, standing there looking after me, as always.

"Ree, let's go home," he said, sounding exasperated.

"No, I don't want to, I don't want to be here anymore. I can't do anything right."

"This is silly. Nobody is perfect. Everybody makes mistakes, and you can't run from your mistakes." I was crying and resistant. Junior became firmer. "Now, let's go! You can walk, or I'm going to drag you back to the house. Either way, I'm not leaving here without you. You're coming home, and you are coming home now!"

And there it was, I could hear it in his voice, that fatherly tone, the professional lumberjack. The words rang out and crystallized the pain and desperation of a boy determined to hold his family together even if he didn't have anyone to hold him together. He paused, had no intention of repeating himself. I could see he was hurting too and that just as much as we needed our father, we also needed each other. I slowly gathered myself, and we walked quietly in the dark towards home. All the while, I could feel God's nurturing presence hovering over our tender souls.

Texas Slim

I was in Junior Reserve Officers Training Corps (JROTC) in high school. It was, by far, my favorite class, that, and commercial cooking. Not even flames in my hair could ruin my love for cooking. Once, my bangs caught on fire when I leaned over the burner to light a cigarette during class. That was just one of many incidents that landed me in the principal's office. But I still earned a full culinary scholarship. However, I started hating high school and forfeited the idea of attending college altogether. But cooking and ROTC kept me occupied and kept me from skipping school most of the time. I loved ROTC because I learned to become a leader and I learned discipline, responsibility, mind over matter, and camaraderie. I didn't feel so helpless all the time.

In ROTC, I also got to hang out with Frank. Frank Corey Shields was the best male friend I'd ever had. I don't know the specific day or when we clicked, but our friendship grew over time. Frank was cool and handsome. The girls were extra giggly when he was around. You know the kind of guy that made you do a double-take in the hallway, that's Frank. Fair-skinned, with a perfect build, he was a dream for any girl. Grandma Pearl nicknamed him "Texas Slim" because she thought he was a "fine young man" and a "tall drink of water," whatever that means. To me, he was just Frank. I adored him, not for his good looks but because he was intelligent and witty. Unlike other boys his age, there was a maturity in him and prevailing kindness that was certainly scarce among high school students.

Frank had a car which added to his appeal with the girls. But instead of baiting in a harem of babes, he took lunch orders for all his friends. Sometimes Frank let me borrow his car to grab a burger or a slice of pizza. I was shocked every time he handed me the keys, knowing I didn't have a driver's license. But he was generous in that way. An attractive guy like Frank could easily be conceited, arrogant, or a dog on the hunt. But he was none of those things. He was a good, respectable guy with a magnetic personality and a whimsical sense of humor. Frank liked me, but he didn't do the "Hey baby, you wanna get with me" stupid thing boys do. He was too much of an old soul for that kind of stuff. He'd just give me the eye, lean over, and strike up a conversation or tell a corny joke.

My talks with Frank were equivalent to cuddling with my favorite comfy blanket. We'd get to yapping, and instantly I was transported in my mind to a sunny day on the beach. Before I realized it, my guard unintentionally lowered more and more every time we spoke. I'd be spilling my guts to him about my father, "I hate my father. He might as well be dead because I'm ever going to see him again." A thirty-six-year sentence was an eternity as far as I was concerned.

"He just went and got himself locked up and left us," I'd continue to lament. Frank would listen with the ear of a well-trained counselor.

"Well, you know," he'd say, "some people just make the wrong choices. It doesn't mean your father doesn't love you," he'd say, erasing any sign of judgment. "He just messed up. When you think about it, he's the one with the short end of the stick." Then he'd encourage me to focus on the positive things in life.

Frank was always present, in the moment, and clung to my every word. The stronghold of his benevolence towered like a forcefield. I was like a fish out of water because I was used to being invisible, suffering in silence. Then Frank came along, unmuted me, and gave me permission to vent and emote. He set my heart at ease. We talked about everything and nothing all at the same time. Being with him was the brightest part of my day. I never understood why he wasn't like other guys. He liked me with no strings attached.

I guess, in part, that was the problem. Frank's goodness was weird and made me suspicious. It seemed wrong, an anomaly, downright strange. How could he like *me*? I couldn't figure out his angle. There had to be a catch. With all the trouble I was getting into at school, my shortcomings were on full display. I wore my rebellion and bad girl behavior like a badge of honor. The noticeable sign was tattooed on my back, if not stamped on my forehead, "Hey, beware, I'm jacked up over here! Proceed at your own risk." But this dream of a guy ignored all warning signs and glaring caution lights. He preferred me anyway.

Frank treated me like a gentle, delicate flower. I found myself exhaling and shutting out the world in the moments we were together. His chaste eyes penetrated through the darkest parts of me. But I didn't know how to be soft or admired. I was addicted to pain. I mostly feared contaminating him, or worse, crushing whatever positive image he had of me. I can't say with any certainty how deeply Frank cared for me, but I admittedly loved him and felt loved by him.

Love is patient, love is kind, love keeps no records of wrong, love hopes, and believes in good. Frank exuded all those characteristics towards me. I didn't have to do anything to earn his friendship, and I certainly didn't deserve or feel worthy of his affection. I could not reconcile the possibility of having a future with him or disentangle the clutch of my father's image that dominated my mind. I had no clear understanding of love in high school. It is a complicated expression when you're a teen. You don't label a feeling as love unless it's accompanied by lust or hormone-induced passion when you're that young. Just thinking that you love someone is usually followed by a commitment to be boyfriend and girlfriend. It meant walking around campus joined like Siamese twins and most definitely demonstrating some inappropriate form of public affection. That's not what surfaced in me. I only felt the pureness and sweetness of his presence.

I was just a teen who subconsciously looked for my father within every male who crossed my path. That's what I equated as true love. Suppose there was the slightest glimpse of my father's characteristics or mannerism in a boy. In that case, that is who I naturally gravitated to. My dad was the measuring tool. Frank had no resemblance to Calvin, Sr., so in my mind, we never had a real chance. My father had hurt me and abandoned me. He was a convicted criminal and yet he was the moral compass and unofficial blueprint for what I looked for in a relationship. Oddly, my father was the standard of what I thought I needed. I was highly manic or subliminally numb at the mere mention of my father's name. So, if I felt crummy when I was with a guy, or if anger or drama was involved, then it was definitely the recipe for love. Once, I saw my father slap his girlfriend. So, if a boy was disagreeable or aggressive, that meant he really, really liked me. Frank was the opposite. He was always in a drama-free zone, consistently above the fray and mayhem of high school. I concluded that he felt sorry for me or was playing the long game to eventually hurt me. When in reality, I was Jenny from the movie Forrest Gump. Frank was Forrest Gump (minus the intellectual disability, Frank was genuinely brilliant). He was my way of escape. But Like Jenny, I was wholly broken, and Frank was entirely untarnished from my view.

I'll never know if Frank and I would have married and danced off into the sunset. But he could have been the beginning of breaking the cycle of relationships with one bum guy after another. Whatever we had, it could have changed the backdrop of my life, the miserable sequel of desperately seeking a Daddy, a tragedy that continuously played on loop. I was trapped in a web of pain and frequent failure. I was still battling in my mind and experiencing things in my psyche that I could not explain or control. But when I was with Frank, my brain was calm. My worries vanished. There was peace and serenity in my complicated being. God planted him in my path during one of the worst times of my life to exemplify what a relationship could be. God showed me light versus darkness, the difference between a good guy versus a bad guy in the most basic form. But I couldn't fully discern, identify, or comprehend it.

Although Frank and I never fully dated, he remained a true friend. We'd continue to talk and go off campus from time to time for lunch. I'd laugh at his corny jokes. He'd periodically remind me of the bad boys that were lurking. "You gotta be careful who you spend your time with because some of these guys are only out for one thing," he'd say with the voice of a watchful guardian. But I wasn't listening. I needed an aircraft marshaller to traffic the bad boys I was entertaining. And when it came to the most memorable moments in my life, like the military ball and prom, Frank invited me to be his date each time. But instead of going with him, I said yes to the drug dealer or someone who wanted me for the wrong reasons. But I was living out my self-fulfilling prophecy and reassured by the toxicity. I knew how to function in dysfunction and had no point of reference for Frank's stable, ethical, respectable world.

We were nearing the end of our senior year, and I still drank and fought. But I managed to work my way up to drill team commander and was forced to clean up my act. Trips to the principal's office and suspension meant I would be demoted. So, I tried to get better at controlling my anger. It wasn't easy. With the constant pressures from my drug-dealer boyfriend and less time with Frank, I was faced with the harsh reality of coping on my own. As fate would have it, I got into another fight. I was then placed on the pending graduation list because of my suspensions. Subsequently, I was demoted from commander to cadet and stripped of all my medals. My mom was disappointed in me. I was disappointed in myself but didn't expect any better of me.

Memory loss, panic attacks, the emergence of an alter ego was getting worse. When my senses were overly heightened or too many emotions started flooding in, my mind and body would shut down. To stave off meltdowns, I trained myself to compartmentalize my life into separate files by simply focusing on one moment or event at a time. No event was related to anything else. No feeling could be automatically transferred or grandfathered in with another scenario. Cross-contamination or cross-pollination of emotions was forbidden. Everything in my life had to fit neatly into a mental file with a clear label, never any shades of gray.

For the most part, I mastered the skill of compartmental-izing, but I'd let my guard down now and again. When my mental files would get mixed up, or if I was jolted from one emotion to another, my palms would get sweaty. I'd feel chills come over my body and then feel as if I was choking. Anxiety would overwhelm me, and I'd start hyperventilating. It often happened after drill team practice when I would wait for Mom to pick me up. I was fearful that she would leave me there, abandon me. If she ran just a few minutes late, my mind would go into a frenzy. *She's not coming. She left you too. You know she's tired of dealing with you. Why can't you be more like your brother and stay out of trouble? You are damaged goods. Nobody wants you.* Then my alter-ego would take over. It was as if Sheria had a kill switch; she knew how much we could handle. The blackout would come next.

But when I opened my eyes, without fail, Frank would be there, smiling down at me, whispering, "You're okay, I've got you. Just breathe." His words rang out as a continuing message from the heart of God.

Letters from Prison

My father began writing me letters from prison. When the letters first came, I didn't want to read them. I was too afraid that he would either try to manipulate me or melt the ice around my heart. I needed to stay cold and numb. It was the only way to survive. I fought to stay guarded, but my rock was fracturing. I picked up the first letter and slowly ran my fingers across the front of the envelope. My mind was racing as I fought back the tears. This was all that I had of my father now. To read the letters meant that I would allow him back into my heart. I didn't want that.

I pulled the envelope close to my chest, crying, fighting the urge to rip it to pieces. Then I looked at it again. His penmanship was beautiful. He had never written to me before. Was he remorseful, bitter, angry? I wasn't sure that I could emotionally withstand the contents. My heart was already steeped in sorrow from just looking at his handwriting. But curiosity got the best of me, so I slid out the letter and unfolded the paper; my tears bled through the ink as I began to read his words.

> Dear Ree,
>
> I know it hasn't been easy for you, and I can't even begin to tell you how much you've been on my mind. It isn't easy for me to feel so far away from you when I want to be close enough to hold you and look at you and tell you with all my heart that everything's

going to be alright. As you move toward tomorrow, may your heart be filled with knowing and understanding yourself and all that is happening around you. As you feel one door closing, may you also feel others opening just for you, and may you feel Daddy's hand on your shoulder, in guidance and encouragement. I'm proud of you, Ree. I want you to stay in school and complete your dreams. You see, Ree, you have powers you've never dreamed of.

You can do things you never thought you could do. There are no limitations in your mind as to what you can be. Don't think you cannot. But, think that you can. Don't ever give up your dreams and never leave them behind. Find them, make them yours and all through your life, cherish them, and never let them go. You know it is a funny thing about life. If you refuse to accept anything but the best, you very often will get it. I'm going to close, but Ree, I don't want you to waste precious time worrying about what you should have done, but rather focus your attention on what you are doing now and what you want to do in the future. Don't concentrate on any mistakes that might have been made but learn from them. Remember, I love you, Ree, very, very much.

Love, Daddy

Incarcerated: Escaping the Prison of Your Mind

P.S. Write to me and let me know how you are doing, please. And I would love to see you.

I became enraged by his false humility and watered-down version of care for my well-being. He's proud of me? He's guiding me? The audacity of him to say these things to me in writing that he should have said to me in person. How could he possibly know how I was feeling? He had no idea how he hurt me and who I had become because of his gross negligence toward me. He couldn't possibly understand my pain or know what I dreamt of being. I didn't have any dreams. I didn't want to be anything and barely wanted to live. He stripped away any hope of a normal life. And now that he was locked behind bars, he wanted to reach for me! I tightened my grip on each side of the letter and started panting.

I sat on the floor weeping and trembling with anger. I grabbed the next letter. What more could he possibly have to say? What mind game was he playing? I snatched the papers from the envelope and was about to rip it from top to bottom when I glanced at the first line and saw "God." I released my grip and began to read with blurry eyes:

Dear Ree,

First, I must say God has been good to me, and I'm very thankful. You know, and I know that without Him, we are nothing. I also have given my soul to God. I've tried everything else, and it didn't work. So, I decided to try God. Ree, He is my all and all. I will trust in Him until the day I die. I want you to know that I love you and Jr. more than life itself. I don't feel bad about you not writing because I understand. I've never stopped loving you. I pray each day and night for you all. I would always worry about you because no one would let me know what would be happening. Your Aunt Mattie would inform me when she would hear from you. Other than that, nothing.

About you and I, we have had some good times and bad times together. But we never stop loving each other as father and daughter. I know it hasn't been easy for you, and I can't even begin to tell you how much you've been on my mind. It isn't easy for me, feeling so far away from you when I want to be close enough to hold and look at you and tell you with all my heart that everything's going to be alright. And I can tell you this, if you keep your hand in God's hand everything will be alright. He will never forsake you or let you go if you trust in Him. Baby girl, I hope you don't mind me calling you baby girl because you will always be my baby. But never-the-less, there are times in every life when we feel hurt or alone. But I believe that the times when we feel lost and all around us seem to be falling apart are really bridges of growth. We struggle and try to recapture the security of what was, but almost despite ourselves,

Incarcerated: Escaping the Prison of Your Mind

we emerge on the other side with a new understanding, awareness, and strength. It is almost as though we must go through the pain and struggle to grow and reach new heights.

Baby, as I have come to the darkest and most difficult moments, it was a signal to the end of troubles and forecasted better days ahead. Our forecast predicts better days. From our saddest moments, we can gain strength, confidence, courage, and the knowledge that a brighter day is just over the horizon. Ree, baby, there is no difficulty that enough love will not conquer; no disease that enough love will not heal, no door that enough love will not open, and no sin that enough love will not redeem. It makes no difference how deeply seated the trouble may be, how hopeless the outlook, or how great the mistake. A sufficient realization of love will dissolve it all. If you could love enough, it would be the happiest and most powerful feeling in the world.

I want you to know that I am very proud of you. I always have been and always will be. Can't no one or nothing ever change my mind about that? I know your mother is proud of you and Junior because she has written and told me so. Tell Junior I say take care of you and your mother and himself. Someday, baby, we'll be together again. If not on earth, then I'll see you in heaven. Whenever you can, come to see me. Please send me some pictures of you and Jr. I don't get very much mail, so to hear from you now and then would mean a lot. So, write when you get a chance, please. Tell your Mom I say hello. Before I close, I would like for you to read this. I read this in a book before, and it said this: this life is yours; take power to choose what you want to do and do it well; take power to love what you want in life and love it honestly; take power to walk in the forest and be a part of nature. Take power to control your own life. No one else can do it for you, take power to make your life happy.

Again, baby, I will conclude by saying don't ever give up your dreams and never leave them behind. Find them, make them yours, cherish them throughout your life, and never let them go. Remember, I love you very much, and so does God. Take care.

Love, Daddy

P.S. Write soon & send some pictures, okay.

How did my father access God's power? And what did he mean he had given his soul to God? He had written his eulogy. He said he was dying to himself. Did this mean he was literally dying? I had so many unanswered questions. I needed clarity about his business with God and wanted to know how my life falling apart was supposed to have meaning. What cruel joke was between him and God concerning me? How could he expect me to look past my botched-up life? He was the broken bridge; he caused the trouble in my life. And as far as I could see, the horizon was dark, and the forecast was tumultuous. I had had enough of him feeding me false hope and scapegoating his guilt through his new God relationship. I decided I would see him, look him in his eyes, and let him have it! I was a teenager and felt emboldened by his detainment. I was going to speak to him in person, and he would have no choice but to listen. I wasn't going to let him have the final word, gloss things over, as if he could just wash away all the hurt with the stroke of a pen.

I decided to ask Grandpa and Grandma Pearl to take me to see my dad, which was in and of itself hard to do. Asking them to take me to the prison made his incarceration even more real. We were at Grandma's house one Sunday after church for dinner, as we usually were. She was cooking in the kitchen, humming. The rest of the family was sitting in the living room watching football, letting their tempers flare, yelling at the television. I stood at the edge of the stove as the steam rose from the pot of mustard greens boiling and felt the heat from the oven pushing the aroma of the pot roast baking. Oil was crackling in a saucepan. Grandma was about to make gravy from scratch. "Sheria, pass me the flour from the cabinet," Grandma always solicited me as her sous chef. It's how I learned to cook soul food. They didn't teach us that in commercial cooking class.

"Grandma," I said, handing her the flour, salt, and pepper. She didn't have to ask. I knew she would need them. "I was wondering," But I didn't speak further. I paused and grabbed a yellow onion from the vegetable basket underneath the counter. I was about to lose my nerve to ask her the question.

"Thank you, baby," She gave a slight grin and a raised eyebrow, a sign of pride and approval that I knew the required ingredients she needed to make good gravy without her having to ask. She continued, "Tell grandma what's on your mind."

"Um, I was wondering if you and PawPaw would take me to see Calvin, Sr."

Grandma turned down the fire on the oil, stepped back from the stove, and wiped her hands into her apron. "Sheria, of course we'll take you to see your father. No matter what he's done, he's still your father. And I want you to pray and ask the Lord to prepare your heart. I know you want to talk to him, Sheria. The Lord will give you what to say when you get there."

It was a long drive to the middle of nowhere. Then the reams of barbed wire and the armed guards from the tower, came into view. The prison facility was massive. I had never seen a prison before and wasn't at all prepared: the oversized doors, the absence of community, warmth, or freedom. Nothing felt familiar. The guards checked my purse, patted me down, and made me feel like a potential detainee. And then there was the long wait to see him. It felt like hours. I wondered what was causing the delay. Perhaps he changed his mind about seeing me, or he was too busy doing something else. Why make me wait for so long? I was growing impatient.

Then a guard finally came to lead me back to the visiting room, and when I first laid eyes on my father, he was barely recognizable. He had gained thirty or forty pounds. There was a tooth missing on one side of his mouth. I was certain he had been in a fight. He was overjoyed to see me and I, him, but we were both different. Still, there was an immediate urge to reach out and embrace him. It had been so long, so many years lost. I wanted to touch my father, hold his hand, or be wrapped in his arms. I didn't want to lash out or hurt him anymore. He was hurting enough. I had gone there with the intention of speaking my mind, but to whom would I be yelling at anyway. The man I knew wasn't there anymore. He had found peace and contentment in prison. Why would I condemn him any further? Wasn't that punishment enough? I felt ashamed of myself. He looked at me with so much pride and couldn't stop grinning from ear to ear.

"Ree, I can't believe you're here, baby, Daddy so happy to see you. You're a beautiful young lady now."

"I'm happy to see you too." I was still overwhelmed with being in prison, my palms were sweaty, I was a little jittery, inspecting everything and everyone around me, but I tried to carry on a conversation. "So, what do you do all day?"

"Well, baby, my daily life is like this, when I wake up in the morning I get on my knees and thank the Lord for sparing my life another day. Then I go to work, and when I come home, I read my daily bread and my Bible." I was lost in his words, looking for some resemblance in his demeanor. I took a mental picture of his eyes, ears, hands, his thick arms, the shape of his head, fascinated by his physical transformation.

"Wait, you work? You have a job in here?" That was surprising.

"Yes baby, I do laundry and other odd jobs. It just depends on my assignment."

"Oh, okay, so what do you do after work?"

"Well, when I watch *The Young and Restless* and *All My Children*," he laughed heartily at himself. "After that I take a nap for about an hour and half. I get up and go play basketball or baseball for a couple of hours."

"Wait, you play sports," my head was reeling.

"Yes, baby, Daddy plays basketball. It's good for us to get exercise, you know." He was a chatterbox. I could tell he was excited to talk to someone from the outside. It had been a while. "Now, after I play ball, I come in and take my shower, read my Bible again, and then I may watch a movie. But on Wednesday Friday, and Sunday I go to church for two hours. Basically, it's the same routine each day."

My original plans were foiled. Instead of laying out my feelings, all I did was learn a lot about his daily life. In many ways, I was relieved because I wasn't at all prepared for the experience of seeing him in prison. The father I used to know no longer existed. I had hated the ghost of years past, an image of who I wanted him to be. I mustered all my strength to stay present at the moment because my mind kept roaming to a place called, "how did we get here." It was all so surreal. No sooner than I returned home, I received another letter from him.

Dear Ree,

After you left Saturday, I sat down and started writing to you. I want you to know that you made my day. I was really sad when you left, but I know you had to go. I really hate that I couldn't hold you in my arms and tell you that daddy really and truly loves you. Ree, you are so beautiful and grown-up now. And I'm very proud of you. If you only knew how proud of you I am. I showed the guys your picture, and they all started calling me father-in-law. They always tell me, old man, you made some pretty children. Then I reply, well, what can I say, when you good, you good.

Now Ree, I don't wonder if I am complete. I know I am. You have made me whole by your caring, your understanding, and love. And in all my thoughts of you today, I felt the joy of our togetherness, security and warmth of the knowledge of our love. Ree, I often think of you and Junior in our distance apart. I remember the times we've spent together and the love we have. These special times are the beautiful memories of my heart and my mind, and I can openly and honestly say that you and Junior are the most cherished in my heart. This separation is only a test, and we know in our minds and hearts that our love is stronger than any outside pressure.

We will always be close in heart together in spirit and love. Ree, when you left, I thought of you not once or even twice, but every few moments, it seemed the memory of seeing you came to mind and my eyes would swell with tears. I need you to stand by my side because it will make my time a lot easier just knowing you are there or somewhere close around. Well, baby, daddy just had to write to thank you so much for coming and to tell you that you are a beautiful young lady. Not only in looks but in spirit also. Ree, please take care of yourself because if anything happens to you kids, I don't know what I would do. I will pray and ask God to take care of you, and I know He'll hear my cry. I hope you will write to me. If I don't hear from you, remember I love you very much.

Sometimes daddy gets weak, and Satan tries to step in. But I say get behind me Satan thus says the Lord. I know everyone has responsibility out there. But to hear from them would make me feel so much better. Your Aunt Mattie writes to me now and then. But long as I have God, everything will be alright. You are a beautiful young lady. Ree, I am so proud of you until I can't say enough words to explain myself. You keep trusting in God and do what's right. Don't give up, because Ree, you have given me more strength and courage to fight on. Tell your brother I say hello, and also your mother. I love you so much, baby, and don't you ever, ever forget that. And never doubt that I love you. Well, Ree, Daddy is closing. I hope to hear from you again soon. May God bless you now

Incarcerated: Escaping the Prison of Your Mind

and forever are my prayers. Take care of yourself for me, please.

Love you, Daddy

P.S. Thank your grandparents again for me, for bringing you to see me.

A War-Torn Mind

The more letters I received from my father, the more I became aware of my own frailty. I had no one to run to, no shoulder to cry on, and no strong arms to hold me. The void of his love could be seen in my eyes, the desperate need to be loved by a man. Men took advantage of the void every time. It seems to be an unspoken law. If you see a girl with no father, she must be taken and abused. She is to be had and used. I believed that if my own father didn't love me enough to stick around and protect me, why would God or anyone else ever truly love or care for me.

It became harder to disguise and conceal my brokenness. I was judicious in my efforts to appear strong as if I didn't need anyone. It was easier to manage my charade than to work through my circumstances. I was prepared to stay broken for the rest of my life because being whole was so incomprehensible. How could I be whole when I didn't have hope that my life could be salvaged into anything of worth. Plus, I had learned to peacefully coexist with my brokenness. There was nothing to fight for or gain by penning my thoughts on false hope. After visiting my father in prison, I was more lost than before. The man I thought I knew and idealized as a child didn't exist anymore. And the new man, the man declaring his love for God, was a stranger to me.

I was truly a fatherless child in every way, and out of pure desperation to belong to someone, I went to God for answers. Whether he would fully accept me or not, God was my contingency plan. My relationship and knowledge of God the Father were growing. I started talking to Him more often through whispers of prayers. My communication was no longer solely based on my pain, but I wanted to know Him as a friend. I kept reading the Word of God and was in awe of the depth and breadth of His being and His love for mankind. The possibility that He truly loved us, loved me, was beyond my understanding.

There were countless nights when I could not sleep, and my mind was racing, so I'd read the Bible or sit in the dark and wait for a sign that God was there. I wanted Him to prove Himself to me. Then out of nowhere, His energy and presence radiated around me, and I would sit awake until daybreak, clinging to every moment. I grew to love our encounters in the silence of the mornings. There was something so profound about waiting in the darkness and seeing the transition to light. It was a constant reminder that God was in control of the earth and everything in it and that the light was more powerful than darkness. In His presence, there was peace, and I could feel the sweetness of God's goodness in the stillness of the dawn.

I started attending church with a new perspective. Instead of acting like a forced spectator, I wanted to be fully present. Suddenly, it didn't matter to me what other people wore, what they were doing or saying. I wanted to access God: His Spirit and His character. I was at a critical crossroads and needed to pursue God for myself, but it was an uphill battle. In my view, God was the one who decapitated my family and amputated my purity. How could I trust him?

The trauma of my experiences left me with a war-torn mind. My perception of life was in ruins, and I didn't know how to build trust with God or where to begin. There was a stronghold on my demeanor, and my toxic thoughts were hard to dismantle. When I wasn't nurturing my psychological scars and wounds, I contemplated ways to retaliate against men. The idea of becoming an emotional predator was stimulating and tantalizing and would keep me in control. But then what would I do with Jesus? My ways were counterintuitive to his teachings, my desires to hurt others and perpetuate toxicity were against his laws. I had no balance in my thought process, no emotional intelligence, only forms of extreme expressions. I was habitually oscillating and walking a spiritual tightrope. Either I was learning to trust God and pursuing healing or forging down a path of darkness that I knew would inevitably end in destruction.

I was sifting through the rubbish of hurt, loss, dreams, and aspirations that never fully developed, and trusting God was not easy, but he was still my contingency plan. My hope was fragile. It didn't take much to throw me off track or draw me back to my old ways of thinking. I struggled between needing control and walking into the unknown with God. The scariest part of it all was I knew to gain God's power, I had to be willing to relinquish my own. To trust God meant that I would have to ignore my suffering, surrender, wave the white flag. I didn't think that was fair.

Then there were the constant nightmares and flashbacks that tormented me and ran through the corridors of my mind. The warfare was nonstop and irrefutable. The bars and chains of sexual trauma and the inexpressible pain of being cut off from my father fueled my fears of the unknown. A life of captivity is what I knew and internalized. I was acquainted with fear and comfortably fettered to rage. Attempting to be free was suicidal and meant that I would need to conjure a measure of hope. I saw no reason to fight a battle I had no chance of winning. So, I acquiesced time and time again to the never-ending war in my mind and remained disconnected, merely existing.

Instead of *being*, I started *doing*. Staying busy was my new way of zoning out. By the time I was seventeen, I had mastered the art of compartmentalizing and learned to cooperate with the alter-ego that sedated me and kept me numb. Pretending to be someone else was the perfect anesthesia. No hurt could get in, no anger or anxiety could come out. It was a warped way of conditioning, but it worked for the moment. Until one day, I realized that I was crippling my relationship with God, and I was inadvertently locking God out too.

Life went on, and my mom remarried again, and although my brother and I had our suspicions about her new husband, we had no time or the desire to size him up, we were busy figuring out our own lives and our future. We were about to graduate from high school and no longer wanted or needed a father. This new stepfather was simply our mother's husband and nothing more. Although he worked for the church, he turned out to be a wolf in disguise, another predator. He was an arrogant, self-serving man, and the local finance clerk.

Because of his dealings with the church, we often visited other ministries. Occasionally, I would run into a friend or someone who knew my mother's husband. One specific friend was a singer I ran into during a local Christian concert. He pulled me to the side to speak with me privately. What he said was shocking, "I heard your mom married the clerk. I sure hope he didn't marry her to get to you." Huh, what? When I asked what he meant, he responded, "You'll see, sorry gotta run, will talk to you later," as he hurried off to join the choir on stage. What an odd thing to say.

It was always my opinion that my mother's husband was a bit of a slickster. He had a sneaky way about him. And he always walked around the house with his bathrobe on like some royal prince strolling about the garden, which I thought was gross, if not strange. But it had been a long while since a man had been in the house. What did I know about what husbands wear when they're lounging around at home? My only objective was to stay out of his way or keep busy as much as possible, avoiding him at all costs.

One day when I was in the backyard watering the grass, I accidentally stood in a bed of fire ants and had to be taken to the emergency room. I was ultimately okay but had a severe reaction of swelling and redness, and the doctor recommended bed rest. I was prescribed medication to combat the pain and subsequent itching. One of the side effects of the medication was extreme drowsiness. The next day, I stayed home from school but decided not to take the full dose of the prescription. I didn't want to be incapacitated and lose my opportunity to take full advantage of a day off from school.

I was resting when my mother's husband entered my bedroom wearing his bathrobe, wanting to check on me. We didn't have that type of relationship. He knew better to enter my room unless I was short of dying. For heaven's sake, it was ant bites and didn't require bedside care. "Did you take your prescription?" he asked. He sat on the bed...

"Yeah," I replied with an attitude. He had a curious look, He knew the medicine caused drowsiness. Later in the day, I took a nap, and he entered a second time, likely hoping I was too disoriented to know he was there.

I maintained the ruse and purposefully pretended to be asleep, praying he would leave. But he didn't leave. This time I did not brace myself and crawl into the cave of my mind. I didn't grab my imaginary guitar and try to block out the moment. I was at a breaking point, tired of being victimized, and was sickened that this man who was supposed to honor and love my mother was attempting to touch me. Enough was enough.

I don't know where the courage came from, but I fought back. I snatched my sheets and spoke firmly and clearly, "What do you think you are doing? Don't touch me!" I screamed with boldness, "Leave me alone and get out of my room! Leave me alone and get oooouuut!" He gave me a smug look. I was furious, and this time I wasn't going to remain silent. I immediately called a family friend and asked her to come get me. She was a God-fearing woman and someone I knew I could trust. I permitted myself to have a monumental breakdown and bore my soul to her. Years of pain that had been bottled up came pouring out. I cried and screamed and cried some more.

When I eventually returned home, I mostly stayed in my room, alone with my thoughts. I wanted to tell my mother what had happened, but the situation was fragile. He was her husband. I was so conflicted. I started talking to God again. Most of the conversations began with, "Why me?" but later centered around my pain, "My heart hurts so bad, please help me. What am I supposed to do?" I was desperate for direction and guidance. I was in a dangerously vulnerable place as I managed and juggled my unruly emotions. This incident had become the catalyst that broke open the dam of my soul, and I didn't know how to plug the hole.

Many nights I'd lament, quietly moan, or plot ways to kill him. But to hurt him was to hurt my mother, and that I could not do. Finally, I yielded to the horror of my experiences, the pit of darkness that was life, and laid it all at the feet of God. "Dear God," I stammered out the words, sobbing, overcome with sorrow. My ears tingled, and the lump in my throat expanded as I, in anguish, pried the words from my mouth, "God if you can take all of this pain away, I'll give you my life. Please God, I can't take this anymore. I don't know what to do. My heart can't take this. I'm not strong enough. I'll die if you don't help me. I can't live like this anymore. Jesus, if you really love me, if you can hear me, please take this pain away. I'll do anything. I'll serve you. I'll never leave you. My life will be yours. Please, please, please make my heart stop hurting."

In my brokenness, I acknowledged my sincere need for Him, my need for a savior and Lord. I laid on the floor sobbing to the point of exhaustion, and then the miraculous happened. God spoke back to me, he said, "You're the one who knows my name, Noel." I later learned the meaning of Noel is "to be born." At that moment, I was born anew.

A Father's Love

My father's letters kept coming, and God the Father spoke to me through them. His divine love began to overwhelm me.

I wasn't a little girl anymore and asked my father to stop calling me by my nickname, Ree, but to address me by the name he had given me, Cecelia. He respected that, he remembered and continued to write.

Cecelia,

By God's grace and mercy, I'm so glad to know everything is well with you. When I saw the writing on the envelope before the boss gave me my mail, tears started coming out of my eyes. The boss asked what was wrong. I told him, "That's a letter from my daughter."

He asked me, "How you know?"

I replied and said, "I know her writing anywhere."

Then he looked at the back of the envelope and asked me, "Is her name Cecelia Simmons?"

I said, "Yes, it is."

Baby, you don't know how I have prayed for you. The Lord has answered my prayers.

Cecelia, I'm so proud of you. More than proud. It's way above the word proud. With God's help you have accomplished what you set out to do. And I know without God's help, you couldn't have done it. Isn't He a good God? You don't have to tell me. I know God is first in your life. Your mother came to visit me, and she told me that you were saved. Hold up the blood-stained banner, Cecelia. Let the world know that for God, you live, and for God, you will die. I want you to know that daddy has been saved. I wouldn't trade God's goodness for all the money in the world. I know one thing: with Him, all things are possible. But without Him, nothing is possible.

I know your mother and Junior are so happy. You are a good child, and you deserve nothing but the best. I know the race was hard, and the run was rough, but look, you crossed the finish line. Now you have something no one can take away from you. They can destroy all books in the world, but what you have within you, the world can't take it away. I want you to know that I'm so sorry I can't be there for your commencement. I want you to know that my prayers and love will be there. I hope and pray that you will feel my presence.

Cecelia, I miss you, and I'm constantly praying and thinking of you all the time. Yet, somehow, I feel that when this separation is over, and we can look on this time from a distance, within the warm security of our love, we will see it not so much as having kept us apart, but as having brought us closer together than we ever were. And we will appreciate more how much we have in having each other. Please, Cecelia, don't ever doubt my love for you because it is as real today as it was the day you were born. Sometimes when I'm alone and sitting in my cubicle, I remember the special times we've shared. Sometimes the memories make me smile, and sometimes it makes me cry. But that's not so bad because remembering what we've already done makes me look forward to the things we've yet to do if it's God's will. But more than anything else, it makes me realize just how much I love you.

Cecelia, thank you so much for sending me the beautiful picture of you and the invitation. I showed everyone here. I think the guys here were happier than I was. I have a lot of Christian brothers here that love me, and I love them. They call me their papa, and I call them my children. The Lord has blessed us so until I can thank God I'm not what I used to be.

Cecelia, Sunday, I want you to stand tall, walk with your head up, and thank God for helping you run the race and cross the finish line. Take care and remember I love

you very much, and so does God. I hope you
write and let me know how the Commencement exercise was. I hope to hear from you
soon.

Love, Daddy

P.S. Write me back soon.

Dear Cecelia,

I want you to know I'm your friend as
well as your dad. If you ever need someone
to talk to, I'm here. You can talk to me
about anything you would like to talk about.
Any time you would like to write, just write
and speak your mind. I've learned that
love is kind and patient, never jealous,
boastful, proud, or rude. Love isn't selfish
or quick-tempered. It doesn't keep a record
of wrongs that others do. Love rejoices in
the truth but not in evil. Love is always
supportive, loyal, hopeful, and trusting.

In other words, love never fails. All we
can see of God is like a cloudy picture in a
mirror. But later, we will see Him face to
face. We don't know everything, but then
we will, just as God completely understands
us. For now, there are faith, hope, and love.
But of these three, the greatest is love.

Incarcerated: Escaping the Prison of Your Mind

Love comes from God, and when we love each other, it shows that we have been given new life. We are now God's children, and we know Him. God is love, and anyone who doesn't love others has never known Him. God showed His love for us when He sent His only Son into the world to give us life. But real love is not our love for God, but His love for us. Let me stop here because I will talk all day. But when I get to talking about Jesus, I'm like Jeremiah (20:9, NIV), when he said, "it's like fire shut up in my bones," and I have to tell somebody.

I really enjoyed Junior last Sunday. He's becoming some man. I'm proud of him, as well as you. Your mother taught you all well. Cecelia, I love you all very much. The Lord will fix everything after a while. Well, take care and remember that you are always in my prayers now and forevermore. I hope to hear from you if you have time to write. I know you are busy, but at the same time, I know you love me.

Love, Daddy

P.S. I thank God for a wonderful daughter like you.

Dear Cecelia,

I'm so glad to know everything is well with you by God's grace and mercy. We have so much to be thankful for. I know I am so thankful for having wonderful children. The Lord blessed me with you all. Cecelia, you don't know what it meant to me seeing you. Everyone tells me they see a glow on my face, one they have never seen before. And you know what, it's all because of you. Seeing you gave me more of a reason to stay strong. You build up so much hope in me. It had been several years since I had seen you, and I thought I had lost you. But now I know you really love me, which means so much to me. I have never stopped loving you and never will. No matter what happens, I will always love you.

I want you to know that God has been working in my life. No matter where we may be or what situation we are in, our life is so much better if we allow God to take control. You have peace, joy, and happiness. But most of all you have love one for another. I'm so glad I surrendered my life to Christ because now I understand God's word where He says, "Do not fret because of evildoers" (Psalm 37:1, KJV) and "Love those who despitefully use you" (Matthew 5:44, KJV). You know it takes God in one's life for them to love their enemy. Now I trust in God and do good.

Now let's talk about you. You have grown up to be a beautiful young lady. You look just like your mother. Cecelia, I'm so proud of you. It's going to get rough sometimes, but with the Lord as your guide, it will be okay. The Lord hasn't brought you this far to leave you. We may leave Him, but He will never leave us nor forsake us. Always remember, the Lord is our refuge and strength. I don't have to tell you these things because I see the Lord in you. I know you are walking with the Lord and He with you. That makes me feel so good to know that you are saved. I want you to know that daddy is saved too. The Lord has taken hold of my life, and I love the feeling. When I come home, what a time you and I will have, serving the Lord together, it just makes me so happy talking about the Lord and especially with you. I pray and hope that you and I write to each other more. I need to hear from you more often because you lift my spirit. I'm so glad that you prayed about your forgiveness. I don't want it to be a division in our family because the Lord wants to be pleased. If we are going to represent the Lord's Word, we must abide by it.

Love, Daddy

P.S. Write me back soon. If it isn't but a letter a month, I will be so happy to hear from you. "May God bless you," is my prayer.

———————————

Hello Cecelia,

Cecelia, God has really been blessing me spiritually wise since I've given back to Him, what He gave to me, and that's my life. I wouldn't trade this feeling for all the gold in the world. I have found peace within myself. I can't wait until I get home so the family can see the new me. I'm so happy, Even though I'm in a place where I don't like to be, God knows what's best for us. My body may be locked up, but my mind and soul are free. And I give all thanks to my Lord, Jesus Christ. After a while, this all will be over. But you know we as Christians have to suffer. Just because we are saved doesn't mean that we will not have trials and tribulations. The test starts when we let Christ come into our lives. The Lord doesn't force Himself on us, but He says, whosoever will let him come. Daddy is going to meet Him.

If it's God's will next year around this time, October, I should be coming home. Oh, what a time that will be. I hope everything is well between you all. Well, Daddy will close here by saying, "May the Lord watch between you and me while we are absent one from another" (Genesis 31:49, KJV) is my prayer.

Love, Daddy

P.S. Write me soon, okay.

He Touched Me Too

With a thirty-six-year sentence, many Octobers came and went. I fully came to grips that my father, Calvin Simmons, Sr. was never coming back. This new understanding was the beginning of a different kind of journey. It gave more room for my heavenly father to operate in my life. I was willing to know him as Father and let Him teach, lead, and guide me. I submitted myself to Him, and with a mustard seed of faith, I challenged Him daily to speak to me and exercise His power over my life, my emotions, and my future. I didn't want to hide anymore or attempt to fix things in my own strength. I was tired, exasperated with trying to make sense of why God allowed me to be so broken. I just wanted to be fixed. Because I was open to His love, I grew in His grace.

I found myself crying often, then cringing at my vulnerability, and crying again, unloading one burden after another, worshiping at His feet. I'd saturate my mind with uplifting and encouraging music my mother raised us on and washed my thoughts in the word of God. Then I did the things I joked about, and thought were silly as a young child. I fasted and tarried privately and stayed on my knees for as long as it took for me to be filled with His Spirit. Sometimes I travailed, allowing the Holy Spirit to speak for me because there were no words that could translate what I felt on the inside. Every time I prayed, I was prepared to wrestle with God until He spoke to me. And in my wrestling, I learned to know His voice and to discern His presence. He consistently and faithfully spoke to me through the scriptures and would whisper reminders of His Word to me throughout the day.

I was in a relationship with God the Father, and He touched me and began to heal me where I was hurting. The most astonishing discovery for me was to learn that God had feelings. God loves, cares, gets angry, and is even jealous. I knew His feelings weren't exactly like mine, but my heart softened to know He understood how I was feeling. I was in awe that He would reveal himself to me in the way He did, gracing me with His presence. His goodness, mercy, and loving kindness toward me consumed my thoughts. There was no stain too harsh, no sin too foul, no stench so pungent that would drive Him away. He wanted me, all of me, and was only waiting for me to invite Him into my messy, chaotic life.

Then it dawned on me that even if I had been born in the perfect family with perfect parents, free from error, I would still need God. We are all born in sin and shaped by iniquity. No one is exempt from needing his sacrifice and love. While some more than others may be predisposed to certain proclivities because of their family's generational curses, we all have a clean slate through the redemption work on the cross. It is the great equalizer. Jesus broke every curse. I didn't have to accept my sinful life or sinful nature.

I had a new life and a new perspective and started the process of forgiving my uncle who molested me and the boys who raped and preyed on me. God's Word and Spirit revealed to me that they, too, were born into sin and molded by iniquity. It's a vicious cycle of hurt people, hurting people. Although I didn't hurt anyone physically, I wanted to bait and destroy men emotionally. I wanted to ransack their mind and destroy their perceptions of love. Had it not been for God's grace, I would be a different type of predator.

The Spirit of God was showing me *me* through His eyes. I wasn't pathetic but had royal blood running through my veins. I had a new beginning naturally and spiritually, adopted into a new lineage with a new legacy and inheritance to latch on to. He promised to take everything I had gone through and make it work for my good. I had never felt so spiritually rooted and free at the same time. My mind and heart were suddenly open to seeing people and life differently. He touched me right where I was bleeding and broken. God the Father ministered to me and to Sheria, the little girl inside who was constantly fighting to protect me. She was relieved of her civic duties. I didn't need her anymore. I was no longer powerless, but I had weapons of spiritual warfare with a host of angels also fighting on my behalf. The thrill of accessing God directly and developing my own personal relationship with Him enriched my spiritual walk. I was committed and full of zeal.

While still a senior in high school, I enlisted in the United States Army at seventeen. I needed my mother's permission because I was underage. I had no plans to go to college, so this was the only option. Mom was entirely on board and could see I was ready to leave the nest. I wanted to serve my country because military service was honorable and made the most sense. I was good at being a soldier in ROTC and was groomed to be a patriot in Texas. God, country, family! I couldn't wait to go away and leave everything I knew behind. I was excited and drawn to the structure and the challenge of the armed forces. I wasn't nervous about going through basic training. I wanted to explore my new life on my own, me and God against the world. How could I lose? I was ready. "I, Cecelia

Simmons, solemnly swear that I will support and defend the Constitution of the United States against all enemies, foreign and domestic, that I will bear true faith and allegiance to the same, and that I will obey the orders of the president of the United States and the orders of the officers appointed over me, according to the regulations and Uniform Code of Justice. So help me, God."

Basic training came with all sorts of challenges, but that was nothing compared to what happened next. I indeed needed God's help more than ever. I was taken into another realm of darkness. My life was hanging in the balance. And once again, God and God alone would be the only source of power that could save and deliver me.

Afterword

Look for the next two books in this series:

- *The Sparrow: Escaping the Prison of Your Soul*
- *Sweetly Broken: Your Pain, His Purpose*

To book Dr. Martin or for press related inquiries, email info@ teemleadership.com or call 1+ (713) 252-1978.

Stay connected with the author and receive the latest updates and travel schedule at: drceceliamartin.com.

Dr. Martin is the owner of TEEM Players Network, LLC & TEEM Leadership Institute (501c3). For more information visit www.teemleadership.com

---

Tell us your story! We would love to hear from you.

Write to:

TEEM Leadership C/O Dr. Martin
634 W Cavalcade Street
Houston, Texas 77009

Email or send a two-to-three-minute video testimonial to: info@teemleadership.com

Follow Dr. Cecelia Martin on:

- Facebook: @drceceliamartin
- LinkedIn: dr-cecelia-martin
- Twitter: @drceceliamartin
- Instagram: @dr_ceceliamartin
- Clubhouse: @drceceliamartin
- YouTube: Dr. Cecelia Martin, PhD

CPSIA information can be obtained
at www.ICGtesting.com
Printed in the USA
LVHW020953070922
727696LV00009B/859

9 781685 565978